March of the Divine Magnificent

March of the Divine Magnificent

H. L. DOWLESS

RESOURCE *Publications* · Eugene, Oregon

MARCH OF THE DIVINE MAGNIFICENT

Copyright © 2020 H. L. Dowless. All rights reserved. Except for brief quotations in critical publications or reviews, no part of this book may be reproduced in any manner without prior written permission from the publisher. Write: Permissions, Wipf and Stock Publishers, 199 W. 8th Ave., Suite 3, Eugene, OR 97401.

Resource Publications
An Imprint of Wipf and Stock Publishers
199 W. 8th Ave., Suite 3
Eugene, OR 97401

www.wipfandstock.com

PAPERBACK ISBN: 978-1-7252-5387-2
HARDCOVER ISBN: 978-1-7252-5388-9
EBOOK ISBN: 978-1-7252-5389-6

Manufactured in the U.S.A.   03/16/20

Contents

The Bonfire Ceremony | 1
The Prophesied Illustrious Emperor | 10
The Ordained Empress | 17
The Hierophant | 32
Behold The Bearer Of Incense | 49
The Swordsman | 60
The Frogman | 79
The Archer | 96
The High Priestess | 107
The Lovers | 118
The Chariot | 130
Strength | 139
Sanctium Munera In Donariis | 148
The Hermit | 155
Wheel Of Fortune | 181
The Hanged Man | 188
Death | 194
Temperance and the rising sun | 198
The Devil and the dark tower | 205
The Moon | 212

Saga Of The Rising Sun: The Delivering Messiah Of The Divine Magnificent | 222

The Judgment | 232
The Blissful World And The Fool | 240

The Exalted Conclusion | 245

THE BONFIRE CEREMONY

High upon
their rippling saddled horses the mighty transcendence rode,
each warrior enveloped in superlative perfection a strode
their shinning sable horses of war;
endlessly galloping forward into the howling midnight wind,
born to make war and
gratify their insatiable lust for blood,
each heart bound up tightly in it's power quest again.

They
poured forward
from the secure depths of their fortress battlements,
to expose their flesh to the possibility of sharp edge
and their hardened bodies to the hazard of
treacherous devices;
like legions of ants they raced forthright from the secure Bastille walls,
rushing forth in an endlessly raging,
intrepid flood,
to fill the souls of mortal men throughout the earth with awe,
and the hearts of villainous women and children with horror
as the once serene emerald earth flowed far and wide
with deep racing rivers of their life blood.

So
rode forward
the brilliantly triumphant nine mil,
to make war with the nether beings
and those among mortal men
bearing their tainted life spring;
for immortal domination was the celestial destiny
of the venerated genetic superlative,

and with the incessant ring of their swords did sing
the timeless voices of divine seraphim,
whom had blessed them with an endless gift
of supreme
intellectual abilities;
it was from them that sprang all positive traits
into the descending blood of men;
the blood of the mortal tainted by corruption
from the elements of earth inside and out,
forcing a descendance from their illustrious superlative
and glittering intellectual clout.

Deep
down into the realm of beasts
motivated only by forces of biology
and environment,
their mutated genes denying them
the ability to make deductive calculation,
their actions doomed to commence in absence of all logic,
answering only to the call of basic physiology
and the compelling extremes without,
born only to do wickedness and
to recklessly poison all of cherished emerald earth about.

For
nine days before,
their endless columns had stood to face
the radiating exaltation of the rising sun;
singing praises unto the unseen celestial phantom within,
who gave them his most generous blessings
and then,
their ears perceived the growing howl of solar wind
far without,

then the distant rolling thunder initiated
the increasing world wide roar of high seas
all about;
and the terrifying voice of the sacred Adonis spoke
unto all his dreadful condemning words,
intending to encourage emotions of both respect
combined with a cold shivering fear,
causing the hearts of the superlative to race
with altruistic confidence and exalted cheer;
for the time had arrived for them all to ride at marching pace,
to redeem the blood of their mortal subordinates
from the grasp of the negative Maharajah extreme,
who had cursed the emerald earth
in his jealous race against the positive supreme,
causing the corroding destruction
of their dynastic children s' superlative gene.

The
poisonous genetic mutations
removing the inheritance of logic
and precious translucent acumen;
hence
so many of them had bred
with those horrendous Stygian beasts,
of whom had so greedily consumed without reason
or any organization in the least,
living only to gratify his own perverted lusts
and biological motivations,
as though those among the lucid to him
were in endless dept and resulting servitude;
and the sable beasts believed that they were in possession of
sanctified permission to pillage and
destroy,

simply on the basis of their sudden need
and the absence in their own tack of ploy
and delightful ingenuity.

High
in the mountain
stronghold of their well watered,
bountiful land,
stood the huge mansion fortress
of those superlative grand;
facing the rising sun
they all stood in endless columns within,
their intrepid leader rising before them anon,
in tribute to offer his embracing words
to their hungry ears in sum,
and the searing foreboding sword
of motivation into their racing starved hearts
and celebrating hoards.
High above their heads he raised
the ominous right handed battle salute,
facing the masses as he spoke his soul piercing words
in exalted praise,
then all turning to face the sun
in dawning resolute
and embrace the perceived verve
but invisible momentum of the magnificent
Adonis within.

Upon
the porcelain floor in their midst
radiated that tesserae
colossal *furvus* emblem of the immaculate sun,
to embrace the spirits of force and

give direction to those warriors once more again,
only to unite with the intrepid phantom
of the astronomical luminescence without,
whose instructions were to proceed forward upon earth
and to redeem her mortal men
from the wicked forces
of those somber corrupted beasts
and the negative Sultan within,
to replace it with the positive gifts of reasoning,
Loyalty and artistic creativity,
with scientific wisdom to supersede all comprehension
of the corrupted mortal intellect,
whose poisoned blood had thus been tainted
with the degrading blemish of the beasts
and the desecrated blood of those whom were never chaste,
even in the very least.

The twelve fires
of destiny burned faithfully
in their sanctified cathedral niches all around,
the ashes of their supreme leaders
encased in graceful inlaid porcelain,
gold, and gem,
only to sit enshrined near
by the dancing bonfire lively beam,
with those of their last glorious absolute leader
in the midst held immortal supreme!

Into
the heavens rode their timeless chanting praises
and cheerful victory songs,
singing abiding hymns of their hallowed triumph,
those exalted psalms of that supreme pinnacle

unto whence they all belong.
Reigning supreme on mortal turf,
born to redeem the blessing of the earth
that the immortal supreme positive,
Caelicola,
bestowed unto them alone,
only to be perverted by the jealous greed of the infernal one,
wrenching the cherished legacy of their realm from the death throes
of their trembling empty grasp.

Now
as they stood round about in great circle,
firm grasping hand
entwined in trembling sweating hand inside and out,
both of those within
as well as all those without;
in their midst burned the sacred flame of oak to announce,
that their predestined time for the earth's redemption
had thus finally arrived all about,
to give their homage unto the supreme superlative positive
of the entire universe,
no doubt,
and to chant their songs of magnificent glory
into the lusting ears of their own,
and to cause tremendous dread to flood
into the hearts of all their enemies
who dared question their precious inherited clout.

On
the stroke of twelve screamed
the esteemed horrendous Banshee to proclaim,
that the time for all consuming world war
had now at long last arrived,

and to renounce
the purloined possession of the earth by the nether mortals
and their abhorrent god-demons who infest
the earth with their putrefying presence,
bearing their only intention to ruination
and destroy
by their unceasing consuming defilement.

Across
the immense dragon's mote
did the massive drawbridge now fall,
and from the twelve mystic directions
came the exalted mesmerizing call,
to ride forward into emerald earth
and to march forth upon all mortal men,
for the purpose of superlative genetic restoration,
the redemption in splendid inheritance
of illustrious intellect,
and to reestablish the precious rule of logic
and legitimate law.

Like
raging hornets
they now all did so forthright ride,
donned in striking battle dress,
causing all of those opposing
who witnessed their enrapturing advance,
to flee in absolute terrifying distress.

Behold,
all of those whom were wed unto the infecting nether-men
did perish first,
saving all of those remaining poisoned descendants

for their later sadistic worst;
their creative imaginations bore no pitying limitations,
for their duty was to conquer;
and for the consecrated blood they were bound to redeem,
their exalted voices in holy unison,
declaring only that
the truest blood of their own descendants
was most certain
TO REIGN SUPREME!

THE PROPHESIED ILLUSTRIOUS EMPEROR

High
above on hallowed podium perfection,
he did gracefully stand so resolute,
his stern face toward the rising sun,
his right hand forward in righteous salute
to the greatness of the heavenly Adonis
and superlative genes of the masses poised in honor filled
tribute;
hail to the greatness of the mighty Supreme in bequest,
for it was through them that the earth did prosper in gold
and their hearts in true love's test,
all creative intellect was inherited through
those positive genetic components in their precious blood best;
all propensity for honor and loyalty,
and the value of industriousness,
skilled crafts,
endowed poets and
those brilliant artists'
elegantly talented impress!

Unto
their gathered masses
he spoke of the exalted god king's coming,
a direct arm of the superlative Lord in consummate,
who was endowed with the supreme command to resurrect.
On his imposing instruction
they were to know
that the earth was given to them by the superlative Lord
and though
the precious birthright from them had been stolen,

that the anointed time had now arrived for them
to embolden;
to make war upon those whom had dared
to question their cherished validity
and to purloin the precious gift that was destined
to be their inherited reality
for all perpetuity.

Upon
his rigid feet were
positioned rugged illustrious boots
of well crafted stag skin,
bearing plush inside fur,
his bare muscled legs
withstanding the rigors of bitter extremities,
as they were.

Upon his torso seal,
firmly wrapped the
well crafted armor of the most elaborate
in polished bronze,
and perfect indomitable
STEEL;
his massive arms were covered in mail
and untainted iron chain weight;
his back strengthened like tempered steel
by constant rigors of the timeless invigorate,
wed with incessant force of grinding wheel.

Upon his right side
he embellished the indomitable venomous dagger,
on his left side
the enchanted sword of the seven raging winds.

In his firm right hand
he carried the lethal javelin of Shamash,
in his larboard hand
the sanctified skull thurible
filled
with the exhilarating beckoning incense,
aloeswood.

Upon his head
was positioned the helmet
of the most immune indomitable steel,
that no metal could slice well
or point could ever punch through.

His voice
was as the sound of the raging seas at tempest,
his body swift as the howling winds without.
For in his mind
he carried the secrets of complete conquest,
and in his heart
he imported the will of incessant persistence;
for the seraphim had conspired to give him
those most cherished in guarded secrets
of the most relished
in unremitting resurrecting essence.

The
exalted force of his will
never grew wane or weary,
for unto his duty
he was eternally bound still,
and of the glow from the golden beacon vividness,
his direction was never cloudy

nor was his sight tainted of dreary mist.

Forward
he swore to move
without backward glance nor wincing hesitation,
into that most sanctified direction,
giving the immaculate Adonis
great jubilant elation.
For now at long last,
the timeless task was to be consummated,
the deed to redeem those most deserving
of the sacred blessings
in revered indefinite
serenity.

Deep
in the wilderness he had begun life,
born in a small cottage by the dale.
His first employment was to harvest the enrapturing herb,
living free of bitter strife
and foul word;
he hunted both the dragon well
and the hart,
skilled in using pups for bear bait
to great avail;
the pursuit was both a task of great endurance
to survive the day
and the skill born from practicing
the ancestral arts.

He dueled
many a bout along the way,
from the academy square right

on down into some secluded field side meadow
or bay;
he learned to master the skills of combat well
and to enjoy the thrills of contest,
when the opportunity presented it self,
as the singing bards always say.

He assumed
a position on high
among the youth who surrounded him
in that long ago valley;
many times he would gaze
backward at those glory days gone by,
pining for the joys of his long lost youth,
and the pleasure
of the dames once held in his sway.

While
yet still a youth,
he had joined the forces of arms,
he had excelled in the skills of the bow
and sword bequeath,
exalted supreme in art
of conquering strategy.

His life
was ruled by the power of logic,
all of his decisions based on sound deductive doctrinaire.
The creative power of the poet
was his greatest form of entertainment,
the power of the brush,
behold,
allowed his fellow comrades

the ability to peer into his very soul.
The sweetest of seductive melodies
endlessly flowed from his fingers
which instinctively knew the chords of harp and lair;
the maidens would swoon all about him,
taking great pleasure
just in running their gleeful fingers
through his long golden hair.

To
engage in sacred battle
was his greatest longing,
to conquer in the name of adjoining village
and cherished nation state;
only to do so in demonstration
of the all mighty Adonis' power throne
and the embellished offerings bestowed upon him to date,
for all of those lords
who gaze forward in wonderment throng
to swoon over in great debate.

By his comrades
he was greatly adored and revered,
and by his enemies
he was both respected
and held in fear,
for the power of his intellect
was awesome
and force in his resolution crystal clear.

THE ORDAINED EMPRESS

His dame
was the maiden from the adjacent village,
Lacedurium,
where the wealth of all the merchants doth flow,
her father was a man of outstanding means
and unto
her bosom many lands did he bestow.

Her name
was the title of the ancient heroine,
Androste
her blood was born of those timeless victors
that the sagas so well know,
her enemies still tell those astonishing tales
of her abhorrent dread
and woe.
The spirit of adventure was her hail,
she feared not the uncharted way,
nor the people who may swell
to block her persistent endeavors
in jealous assail,
neither the ax-man nor the swordsman's rise
could from her majestic intentions cause quell,
nor succeed in her making sway.

Even
those mighty men,
skilled in the sacred arts of lethal combat,
came to fear her very presence
if they were known to differ with her intentions,
not a single word of contest in her presence

they dared to say.
She was known
unto her enemies
for her merciless unrestrained imagination,
she was feared by both the great warriors
and those common men
of the fields and hay;
for if one was to challenge her
to battle contest
and lose,
his own family would thus be forced
to consume his boiled flesh,
and the tender flesh of his children
served to their own shivering mother too,
washing all of it down with cold,
though sometimes tainted,
amber tinted stream water;
being denied all wine
during the course of the jaded feast,
or strong booze for
the purpose of dulling the disgust
and pain,
that those sorely defeated
might endeavor to use.

According to legend
her greatest pleasure
was in resurrecting the bronze bull,
into it's bosom her terrified nude enemies
thus were thrust.
The door above their heads being locked,
the merciless flame lit
beneath his belly would cook incessantly,

the victim could only scream
his blood curdling cry for assistance;
for the gracious Queen
the bull's bellows would affectionately
transform
the screams
into a debauched soul enrapturing,
transsentual melody.

At
the doors opening,
the perfectly bleached
bones would astonish
all of those whom would dare to squint
and look.
The brilliant calcimine
of their bones
crafted fantastic dazzling jewelry,
the haunting memory of their names
for all the ages
now made known.

Into
battle totally nude,
forthright
she boldly rode,
blocking both spear
and sword thrust upon her,
delivering her
the proper returning
death blow.
Soon the heads
of her enemies

would heap surrounding her bosom,
causing many to flee
in great dread
and woe;
for it was always said
that beneath her edge spring
a thousand fold did fall once,
and of her decorated valor ring
their magnificent legends still doth sing,
and of her heroic honor
all their people still doth know.

In her life
she had held many dazzling titles,
and of those fantastic adventures
did her gifted intellect
endeavor to know,
for she hath been
the lover of many great kings,
and the adventure
was found in the weaknesses
of their kingdoms;
hence
the strategy for their conquest
deduced from hidden knowledge.
On most occasions
her conquest occurred
without her ever needing
to exit the mansion palace;
thus
it was always said
that she had achieved the maximum apex
in strategic military accomplishment!

On
those occasion
that she needed her armies to advance,
they knew specifically
where it was that they were to first strike,
causing the opposing armies to crumble before her;
nay,
delivering the wealth
and land into her lusting bosom,
and all trembling opposition
underneath her merciless sway.

Now
many kingdoms did she hold
and boundless wealth
was hers given unto her every whim,
for the prophesied leader
her delicate hand was golden,
even though her embellished reputation
was more one of the villain;
Behold
for the illustrious leader
to even consider her matrimony,
then he himself
must indeed be both
cleaver and bold!

But
the command of the Holy Adonis
must be held in the absolute,
the marriage he would thus
hold at bay;

the words of the prophets
must be exalted
and revered;
let the Queen alone
suffer the wrath
of the mighty Adonis
without any hope of restitution,
if she should ever
turn and stray !

His
accomplishments were outstanding,
the enemy thus
from him did flee in great haste;
his force of arms dominated the field,
his limbs craved
the feel of the divine steel,
his eyes craved
the sight of their ripped bodies
lain to grisly waste.

The
desire for total conquest
rode supreme in his mind;
the taste for their blood
born intense on his tongue,
his empire bore his solemn desire
to reign in ultimate supreme,
with that of the enemies' lain to waste behind.

The
forlorn filthy culture of the nether-men

he endeavored to permanently expunge,
by outstanding conquest
he lain many thousand thousands
to waste on the fields of the ancient hectacomb.

The earth soon lusted
for the sweetness of their infected blood,
shed by the finely honed edge
of indomitable steel;
yea
the heavens high above
shall taste the sweet scent of their flesh
rendered flying by the dancing flames
of the marvelous midnight bonfires,
and the brute force of their
unconquerable will.

So
thus he was chosen
by the immaculate Adonis' cardinal decree,
both he and his beautiful bride to be,
they were chosen to stand
in reigning apex above the nine mil,
for both they and their genes
were perfectly unadulterated still.

Their
revered fore-bearers
had done them great favor
in homage to their exalted past,
to persist in separation
from the once
enchained nether mortal kindred,

declaring that far from among those beasts,
of their own kind should they
forever remain in
supreme caste.
The gift
of comprehending freedom
and the ability to function
within it's limitations,
stood far from the ability
of the nether mortals to intellectually grasp.

But
the sympathy of those
among the transparent consanguinity
had caused them to backward cast
even their own youth,
giving up their own freedom
and kingdoms,
giving up what the immaculate Adonis
had so benevolently granted
them back in those distant ages past.

The
demon possessed leaders
of their own lucid kindred,
forcing even their own youth
to taint the cherished pedigree,
even in the very face
of the enraged Adonis above,
surly as the wrath of his motivated anger
poured upon the land
as a cleansing flood.

The
howl of the winds raged
to announce his anger,
as did the unremitting waves
of the seven seas,
the thunder of the distant mountains
all across the face of entire universe,
the belching magma from her sacred bosom
surged to consume all life';
so it will thus be,
and many thousand thousands perished
in the wake of his rage;
thus still
didst the base debauchery continued to occur,
even into this present age.

First
came the great mudslides
to the far west,
in those distant lands
of the Mayan kingdom;
even though a mil
innocent perished
amid their forlorn deterioration,
they attenuated by forces
of their incessant corruption still.

Then
came those massive floods
upon the heart of the continent,
with that colossal harvest of death
they did take.
This followed by the tremendous tsunami

in the Malaysian wake,
and a million more into the dust
did those dreaded waters make.
To the far west
lay the invincible kingdom
where the center of all depravity now stood,
so the immaculate Adonis
allowed those ancient lords of war
to shake her foundations as best as they could.
Even in the deaths of thousands
the wickedness within her boarders
still continued forward
from whence it then stood;
in the face
of the disgraced Adonis,
they still carried on in those lies
bearing their evil innovations,
just as he knew they would.

Their
people had enjoyed an outstanding abundance,
for the immaculate Adonis
was most grateful and merciful,
since they had been the savors
of his chosen ones,
resurrecting their cherished kingdom
in the land of their patriarch fathers.

But
that fateful day of atonement
was sure to arrive,
for they all were guilty
of the unpardonable sin

of insulting the kindness
offered down unto them by the Adonis,
and blaspheming his holy name
even to the very end.

In
their academies the lies
were forced
upon those impressionable minds
of their most innocent youth,
those lies that defy all logic
standing
in total rejection of the perfect truth.

For
by his immortal hand
they had all been fashioned
from brilliant light and dust of the earth;
with his own breath
he breathed the wind of life into their flesh
and lungs,
and by his hand alone
were they all given birth.

By
their own blasphemous declarations,
they had rejected him
and their own
superlative translucent kindred past.
In his place
they had chosen a base doctrinaire,
that choosing to believe
in an inferior caste

ascending into a superlative heir,
due to the corrupting forces
of time and nature,
while ignoring the absolute truth,
that corruption can only lead into a tainted wear,
bearing the intellectual capacity
of the entire species cast
into the base realm of mindless beasts,
as does the effect of bloody meat cast
before the feet of a starving bear.

First
in collapse was their
illustrious economy,
due to the dark extortion
of their own treacherous leaders
who pursued their foolish financial doctrine
without cease or right,
for the solemn purpose of supporting
the now luxuriant lives of the nether mortals
and the purgamen,
even to the detriment
of their own cherished right
of individual enterprise.

Next
came the collapse of their morals
and the encouraged hatred of men
toward the love of dames who are chaste,
in favor of the abhorrent sodomite perversion,
in spite of Gomorrah's' flaming brimstone destruction;
for the wrath of the mighty Adonis
never makes wasteful haste.

Soon
the gratis awards came a calling,
the eyes of the barbarians
followed the beaming beacon,
their colossal hoards
from those dismal distant meridian lands poured forward,
streaming across the cherished virgin heartland,
bearing secret intentions of destruction,
by first bleeding the coffers
of the compelled masses dry;
then
when the monstrous masses
had firmly settled,
their dark plans for conquest
would abruptly reveal themselves
unto their astonished opponents,
who could only stand by
in staggering disbelief.

Their
wages plunged,
with the barbarians now
in the numerical majority;
their people staggering out into the dismal streets,
now rendered homeless,
destitute and starving,
their will to labor as servants
in abject subjugation to the magisterial corporations
was non existent;
those that labored
still dwelt in dark cardboard slums,
their children crying wails

of hunger and distress
with the hearts of their parents
torn asunder,
for their imaginations could devise
no effective solution,
and so their resolutions
were to simply tolerate the horrid conditions,
longing for a shinning leader
in whom they could place their absolute faith,
only to him offer their unquestioning loyalty
and altruistic commitment
unto the cause of their hallowed redemption.

Behold,
unto all the earth
they shall endlessly sing
their song of forlorn sorrow,
for their situation was caused
by those bleeding hearts
who only stand by in idle apathy,
serving only by asking idealistic questions,
bearing the insidious intention of neutralizing
any forthcoming action that
might admonish the horrible situation,
and reestablish the translucent blood
of those most hallowed exalted elites.

Hark!
All of ye dark demons
who stand by in idle oblivion
and only speak vanities,
for the almighty will
of the immaculate Adonis

is unquenchable!
The brute force
of his active hand invincible!
His plans will never relinquish;
the negative intention
of the bleeding hearts
simply just play a part
in the supreme strategy
to reclaim all
that which was thought eternally lost;
so that those chosen saints could sing of the glory
in those long lost days of majestic yore,
when the rule of intellectual enlightenment
and wealth reigned
as sanctified and supreme,
and the nether mortals
were in complacent servitude unto
those who were most deserving of entitlement,
determined through ceaseless initiative
and the blessed virtues of supreme endeavor
and intrinsic artistic creativity.

HURRAH!
Unto all of Thule earth.
For thy sanctified leader
hath been already chosen,
thy redemption shall cometh
upon thy bosom in an instant,
thy rude oppressors shall soon feel their horrid fate
for the duration of an intrinsic eternity,
and their torturous prison shall
thus endure
for the timeless span of a perfect infinity!

THE HIEROPHANT

or

(the prophet)

His
blessed robe of silken white
was extoled by the heavenly spirits
and those most holy saints on high,
his flowing beard of sandy gold,
was immaculate,
and forever among the wise
doth his gracious counsel lie.

In
his right hand
he carries the timeless golden chalice
of the immaculate
Zorothrausi,
the wine of his omniscient knowledge
forever desired
by all those who bear the wisdom of it's sacred existence,
and of the ability to conquer those perplexities of life
and persevere in a most prosperous direction,
by which one is ultimately certain to go.

In his heart
he carried the spirit of adventure,
and in his mind he carried the wisdom
to relinquish all fears of insecurity,
developing the precious skills to succeed were
thus his only indenture.

Before him
in the majestic courtyard,
he burned those mighty fires of hallowed oak
ere the colossal multitudes
who praised him,
requesting the sacred direction
in which they all should forthright go.

He
gazed steadfast into the dancing flame
and the smoke,
beholding those ancient spirits
who spoke of their predestined greatness
and how their justified anger
toward their enemies should grow,
until it propelled their motivations forward,
but only by proper strategic plan,
for all their efforts were designed to trample
their oppressors beneath them,
and
resurrect their superlative position
in their sacred promised land.

BEHOLD
He held both hands high
to adorn the fantastic spirits of the dancing midnight flame,
he sang jubilant songs of praise unto
the immaculate Adonis.
He
lusted for the power of ancient kings
and
those outstanding lords
of superlative battle strategy;

he knew well from whence
his motivated direction came!
The compulsion that appeared
with the unison chants,
indeed,
were much more
than the mortals' ability to forbear,
for the absolute truth in their words
was so apparent;
behold the lies of the destructive demons
held no substance,
their mass becoming clear as
unblemished crystal,
for the victims now saw that the
tainted demonic intention
was to destroy them by generations
of forced nether-men desecrated heirs.

Their
method of coercion
was to publish obvious lies repetitively,
poisoning those impressionable minds
of their youth,
telling fantastic fables of nether-men grandeur,
when the obvious once betrayed the fable
as a sick twisted lie,
in that it could never measure up
to what was standing before them
as a most glaring truth.
Only those fools
and the scourge among their own kind
could never decipher,
only to give in to the tainted debauchery

pushed by those demon possessed leaders,
forever thrusting forth those base desires
of the most uncouth.

GOOD RIDDANCE
to all of them and their tarnished inferior kind
who forbear our company!
Desiring instead to dwell
within the purgaman squalor
and depravity,
eternally consumed in their disgusting,
sickening debauchery.
Permit them simply to waste away
into the consuming void,
when their dreadful day of atonement
shall surly manifest!

Relinquish
the repressive forces of government regulation,
Oh our majestic one,
allow the might of nature to reign in it's stead,
then all the earth shall behold the truth
in the natural order
and only by it be led;
when the chaff shall separate from the wheat
by the natural force of the wind,
indeed;
and by intrinsic force of gravity
and a simple water well,
shall the nut
thus
separate from it's clinging shell!

The
waste shall thus be cast asunder,
and only then the cherished inheritance
shall rise into it's predestined position,
their iron studded boot soles on the necks
of the mindless nether mortals
via the help of the universally venerated cherub,
as their sanctified singing praises
unto the immaculate Adonis sublime
for all henceforth ages
shall tell.

BEFORE
the raging flames
the prophet held his hands
thrust high into the heavens above,
giving homage to the spirit of *Anunn*.

BEHOLD!
In his mind he acknowledged forthright,
that he by his own
held no special skill,
but only stood forward
as the embellished medium
through which those ancient gray ghosts
could bestow their imposing will.
For security and protection in battle
he prayed to *Sin*,
who upon freely offering his voice
of instruction and protection,
counseling him to ease forward in supreme demonstration
of intrepid faithful allegiance
to the truth in his illuminating words.

Through
the roaring flames
he stood alone
to speak the words aloud,
only to be carried forward by the smoke
and the winds to the ears
of their illustrious leader,
who shall act on complete security
of the spoken logic without question,
or pause
in doubting hesitation.

Gradually
toward the roaring flames
he did move,
speaking those words
of sanctified instruction,
only to render the looming doubts
of the faithless asunder,
motivating the conquering spiritual energies to prevail!

Both
hands he thrust into the heart
of the roaring flame,
to the gasping shock of the masses,
whom by their very surprise
only demonstrated their doubt
and consequential lack of faith,
betraying their unworthiness to triumph.

Forward
the prophet moved continually

until his next step carried him
into the very heart of the intense flame.
Though the great fire
leaped all around him,
immune to the heat
his clothing and body did remain.

BEHOLD
He stood tall amid the searing cinders,
thrusting both hands high
towards the heavenly midst.
His body and health
was with him,
his soul and his spirit
were still glued.
Towards the heavens
he raised his solemn face
screaming those words of petition into
the high heavens
and the seat of the spirits,
solemnly requesting that the people
remain faithful and true;

"Oh my illustrious
Ahuramazda!
Thy sacred words of instruction
so strait and true,
From whence
shall our immaculate savior,
Zorothrausi
cometh,
and from what directions

shall our future actions
proceed unto?

On
what grounds
shall we first advance forward
toward our sanctified liberation,
to best render our enemies into the booted dust asunder
and give restitution
to our lucid blood and
our divinely promised nation?

Breathe
thy words of hallowed instruction
into our lusting ears
, and hearts
before our precious blood
and nation
is consumed by our horrid abduction
and tears. . .

Oh my immaculate
Zorothrausi. . ..,

from
the far south
those treacherous heathen hoards
do come,
from the far east the vanara-men
do surge with them,
only to do their bidding
until the time our vast resources vanish
by all of their

wasteful thefts
and outright plunder,
and then,
of the five life giving elements
we have none!

Was
our cherished land
not your gift for our dutiful service,
both unto you
and thy heavenly name?
Was not our gift of wealth
and high standard of living
not your award for placing ye
upon our most cherished pedestal,
is it for our inherited greatness
that upon you,
the wicked ones cast forth
their envious blame?

Behold,
Oh my consummate twain. . ..!

I
observe them
as they launch their base attacks
upon thee in thy honored place!
I
observe them when they strike
thy venerated name from
our cherished text books,
replacing them with their infected lies
and ridiculous claims,

debasing our lucid history
and posterity
in the minds of our cherished youth,
encouraging them to resent our precious heritage
and our honored face!

Oh
dear great ones. . ..,
they tell those horrid lies
to pass them off as truth,
wrenching the glory from our past accomplishments,
attempting to elevate
the vanara-men into a perverted glory,
forsooth!

I
behold them as they strike
thy precious name from our pedestals
and podiums,
only to replace our hard won morality with
an evil twisted perversion
that is both abominable
as it is uncouth.

HARK NOW. . . . .!
I beseech thee to lash out
in thy complete rage,
smash them all into mere bits of rubbish,
mere food
upon which the feral swine may graze!

Destroy
their nits in the bellies of their bitches,

please spare all of emerald earth
the scourge of their pathetic race!
May their putrid bones
become food to the rats
concealed in their stony niches,
may their presence now eternally melt
from before all our faces!

Oh
my majestic ones on high....

I
behold their vain nether mortal leader,
who by the vanity of our own traitorous shepherds,
was allowed to assume
our once untarnished throne!

I
observe him
as he strikes thy cherished name
from our supreme palace,
as he falls prostrate in homage
before the feet of great villains!
How dare him....!
Unto our pitiless opponents
he designs to sell out our future generations,
enslaving them
to newly prospering nations,
only to serve dutifully
while shedding their wealth for
for the prosperity
of other distant kingdoms!

Allow
us to redeem thy scourged covenant,
repositioning thy lost glory
and thy fame,
then,
offer us forth
the promise of an
all consuming,
climatic victory battle;
please allow their blood
to pour freely forth
from our freshly honed blades.
We now ask all of this
in thy precious eternal name,
Amen."

The
prophet transcended
from the searing flames untouched!
The spirit of his prayers
remained true unto his faith,
not even a single hair was singed
in as much!

Forth
from his clothing
gray smoke billowed upward,
though he stood before the masses
speaking those words of truth,
the evil around him tainted the earth
in his shocking wake;
the plans had formed
and thus

given forth from the mighty spirits for the take;
he made his address
unto the unblemished leader
of the mighty superlative army,
offering forth those words of instruction
born from those ancient gods
of fire and struggle;
the great
Zorothrausi
blessed the holy endeavor,
the conquering Lord Of The Superlative
would surly reign for all eternity,
his great Lordship
had been preordained by the primeval sages;
so the famous prophet
now stood strong before the massive crowd
standing poised in their battle formations,
speaking those inspiring words
that were destined to redeem the holy sacrament
of true blood
and their lucid nation.

"Ride
forth thou enthroned Superlative,
do boldly ride,
into emerald earth to seek battle
from thy dark oppressive demon
that can no longer be denied.

Slash
with thy sword
and chop with thine ax,
until the infected blood floweth

and the vile spirits flee screaming..,
destroy the twisted flesh
until their tainted life stream shall
thus,
greatly lax into
into a perfect infinity!
Then
among the vanara-men
our precious generations shall
no longer abide,
the infected heaps of their putrid flesh
shall be thus
consumed by our colossal zealous flame;
thus
the precious integrity
of the free earth
shall for ever be maintained.

Oh
thou great ones
of majestic valor. . ..,
with exalted jubilation
do boldly ride forth!
Proceed
forward without further ado
in the direction
of the strongest four winds,
commence thy march in massive streams;
first from the great North,
for thence lies
much less of the blighted blood
to make amends.

March
forward in great strength
of both body and mind...
toward the dreary South,
from thence the nether mortals
in frantic disorderly haste
shall surly move forth;
but alas from the east
we shall strike in silent stealth,
merging while asserting
our illuminating dominance
from their rear guard for our sport;
but from the West
our most gifted warriors
shall trample them underneath
in our overwhelming best,
until the entire earth shall then bow
unto our illustrious superlative might,
only to beg for our mercy
in the middle of that most spectacular night;
in our perpetual service
they all shall find the answer to their prayers,
singing loudly those sweet songs
of exalted homage
and adoration,
unto the omniscient Lord of all lords,
Ahuramazda,
and his altruistic son,
Zorothrausi!"

Should
they all dutifully labor
on our sacred kingdoms' behalf,

their greatest honor
shall be the opportunity
just to demonstrate their patriotic fervor,
to simply hold the cherished flag
up by its glistening oaken staff,
to march forward in our great honor
and only to discover
the simple pleasures
of their life's total dedication
unto those most deserving of the sublime
honor;
only then may they breed
to more in our service make,
for our fears shall then no longer lie
concerning our precious resources
that they might endeavor to take.
The heavenly atonement of the promised land
shall thus be ours for all posterity,
to shine forward in radiating glory
for all time into
perpetual infinity!

BEHOLD THE BEARER OF INCENSE

By
the prophets side he stood
tall and strong,
as the mighty winds commenced to toss,
for the fervor of the spirits had vastly increased
and were thus at no lose;
he faced the fury of the midnight winds,
raising both hands high
unto the now stormy heavens,
as the words of the prophet were spoken
and the force of the vengeful spirits was unleashed;
for the wickedness of all the earth
they sought to dislodge,
and the sins that they endeavored to dissolve
were the entire grotesque seven.
Since
the very dawn of all time
they had been the scourge of all positive heaven,
only the tools of the dark one
who sought to dis-leaven,
the precious creation of the positive on earth
with the seductive
lure of those bane seven.

Into
the bronze skull thurible
of those ancient revered
priests on high,
was placed those sacred herbs
that induce eloquent exhilarating visions;
behold all mankind

the timeless power of the gods,
to prevent daunting destructive divisions!

First
goeth the herb of dark lavender,
belladonna,
to free the mind from all perplexing thoughts,
and imbue the cherished intellect to envision total victory;
now
beholding the succulent flesh
as it shall part from their fine swords,
and the flowing rivers of villainous blood that shall
fall from their honed efforts;
and naught
shall they suffer
but only receive those sanctified blessings,
pouring forth in honored torrential floods!

Next
goeth the precious
blood-root,
for all vexations cured,
most prevalent being field fevers and
those rancid skin infections
that all warriors must endure.

With
all gentleness goeth the
wormwood,
to purge the blood of it's infected evils
that time hath thus wrought,
and to render
the enemies' vile poisons

into a discouraging
naught.

Now
in shall go the
mandrake,
to render the pain
of enemy blows all
in vain,
with which to purge the open wounds,
to ensure our victory
just the same.

In
honor to the spirits of healing goeth the
mistletoe,
offering strength unto the blood
of our warrior heroes,
to eliminate all those
wicked vices that the lord of darkness
might bestow.

In
shall go the
hen-bane,
to
render the corrupting forces
of the march in vain,
so that the shear power
and bedazzling speed
of their massive booted thunder
shall
never slacken

nor grow wane!

So
shall follow the precious
frankincense,
when our illustrious heroes shall
suffer their fate in death,
now their corpses
be born for eternal honor,
and their revered places
of infinite commemoration shall,
thus,
their elite descendants
know best!

Now
thy days hath darkened
and the winds shall howl throughout,
the low rumble of distant thunder
rules the skies,
and thus
the blue fires of our raging gods
shall flash all round about!
Upon
the high pedestal,
before our illustrious leader,
he takes his gracious stand,
fire streaks all around him
to announce the Superlative Grand!

Forward
in tight fist,
he thrusts the thurible above,

his radiating assistant
shall then
alight the mixture in love.
Force
of the increasing winds
seize the caliginous mixture,
racing across the mass of coordinated warriors
from their loft high above.
With
the breaths of the warriors
who righteously stand
with their eyes now fixated
upon our illustrious leader so grand;
they now behold those glorious visions
of our forthcoming victory,
that are destined to be repeated
across our promised earth land!

Through
the imposing veil
of the distant yon mist,
their eyes now behold the precious Superlative
without any indecisiveness.
Now
their minds shall know
of their duty well,
that it was them
whom were born to conquer,
those extravagantly gifted ones
of whom those most ancient of sagas
do tell!

From
the splendor of the heavens
they were thus born to rule,
their glorious for-bearers lived their blessed fate,
setting up expansive colonies
that have been unequaled to this present date.

From
those distant plains of northern Sinea,
they once ruled without abate,
a mighty warriors' empire
they did endeavor to create!
Onward to consume
and dominate northern
Aryavrata,
blessing the kingdom with their
illustrious creative offerings,
expanding their indomitable sensational Empire
in their wake!

From
these Superlative warriors
spawned
their jubilant children
to thrive in those enlightened days,
from there all the way to
the ice of Scandia,
was once
held in their cherished sway!

Mighty
men of idolized renown,
they were,

of accomplishment
and stature divine,
eternally prospering in the life
of a most elegant in luxury enshrined,
that by their own strategic industry
did they artfully
design!

The
cherished knowledge of wine
was their grand blessing to the green earth,
and the skill to organize
and construct,
to create those mighty cities of yore
and to give birth
to all future wisdom
and scientific invention,
that even the wisest of men still endeavor
to search!

Many
among them,
some ten feet tall they stood!
Towering high above their subordinates,
just as the all knowing,
Ahuramazda,
knew that they should!

Their
artistry was illustrious,
their craftsmanship knew
no equal among men;
their logic crystal clear,

and their rise guaranteed when
they were confronted
by any nether mortal oppressor,
only destined to vanquish again. . ..
and consequentially on that basis. . .,
. . . . .AGAIN!

Their
reddish golden mane was flowing,
their graceful capes were grand,
their flesh was superbly fair
and unblemished,
my Superlative ipsom men!
With
their enemies all knowing
that not a single one of their endeavors
or silent contemplation,
could aspire to proceed forward,
intending to bear
the majestic art of surprise,
since they could never escape
the piercing sapphire
of their omnipotent eyes!

Thus
their kingdom was vast
and no limitations knew,
their superlative rule was logically just,
and so their prosperity righteously grew.
By the ancient sagas
their story was destined to prevail
into those very distant generations
of wise men,

who knew well
of their greatness
through genetic observations,
those perfectly preserved corpses
bearing the solid proof
where their progenitors could ensue;
the secret wisdom
that they deduced
through their majestic metaphysical adventures,
and those timeless tales
of their ancient greatness
that their adoring children shall seek to woo!

Hail
my precious immortal children!
Ye
honored inheritors
of all emerald earth!
From
those lofty heights of high heaven
ye fathers came,
and hath graciously granted thee birth;
thy timeless employment
engendered to dispense their superlative wisdom
and spread their divine fame!

Through
the rising smoke
of our hallowed yule alder,
doth my enraptured weeping eyes behold,
the glamour and beauty
of those enlightened days untold;
the wisdom found

in their investigative search
for virgin knowledge,
the foundations based upon
the purest of perfect logic,
for with only their minds
the source
of the self evident
manifested found;
thus,
their thorough conquest
of mortal earth
was spiritually destined as
most progressive
and sound!

THE SWORDSMAN

Within
his mighty right hand
the swiftness in supreme skill lay,
woe unto the many thousand thousands
in the vast forthcoming onslaught
that he shall surly slay!
Forward toward him the mounted riders
and the chariots shall be led to move,
but the secret power lay within his blade,
and of his opponents he is certain to undo.
Allow their cries for mercy to ring forth endlessly
unto all the ears of thy cherished earth,
for their villainous bodies are destined to lay wasted,
forever sealing them from any new birth;

BEHOLD,
the Magnificent Superlative
will then be forever free from their rancid curse!
Aye,
it shall be he
and some ten thousand skilled
and strong,
destined do sacred battle with the evil enemy
for the duration of a twelfth year dreadfully known,
if fate should allow the prophesied conquest
to take that long.
As
the scourge of the vanara-men
relinquishes its sable hold
from the throats of all mankind
far and near,

the glittering eyes of all those blameless precious
will never shed a single tear!

Hosanna!
Hosanna on high!
Hurray!
Glory to the Lord of the highest!
Blessed be the name of almighty God
in an outstanding show of thanks for this hallowed day!
Into the dust of the earth
allow that scourge of all the universal realm to fade,
allow their putrid memory
to completely absorb into the dark misty shade
of long wasted time!

Through
the blustery whirl of fluttering
oaken leaves. . .,
I perceive
the divinely appointed conflagration. . .,
I can perceive
the screams of their
vanquished!

Hark!
I can hear the tinkle
in the chains of their conquered captured!
I can feel the exhilaration
in their predestined subjugation!
My eyes can behold
the fruits of their guided labors amid the
wealth produced by our glorious trade
of their production;

only their best
we shall allow to breed
to produce the supreme
in ultimate service to our economic need.

T*HUS,*
forth from the earth we eliminate
their baneful contamination,
of both immaculate island lands,
constitutional guaranteed freedom,
and their base corruption
of our once illustrious metropolis nation;
their non productive filth
contaminating our laboring landscape
into a putrid abomination,
their base nefarious organizations
threatening the precious security
of our entire kingdoms' station!

Forward
we shall ride in supreme
glittering superlative brilliance!
Our
destiny is to avenge those
who forsook
our cherished freedoms' heritage,
HENCE,
only to replace it
with that most repugnant ancient
alien Moorish thralldom
and it's subjugating circumstance!

Hear ye now,
oh ye valorous men of earth!
We men
of free birth
never endorsed this baneful replacement,
but were forced
to endure the wicked imposition
of this repulsive servitude forced upon
the superlative majority,
simply in the name of accommodation
unto those who failed to
sufficiently function in the realm
of the superlative free nation!

Behold
ye warriors for the superlative spirit
of free earth!
Their nether mortal masses
we were forced to acclimate unto,
allowing their incompetent hoards
to step forward before us
in the name of accomplishment,
only for us to secure
at best,
a second class state
in our own predestined
forthright divinely anointed kingdom!

I
witnessed the supremacy of manhood
wrested from the right of men,
in a baneful attempt
at allowing the persuaded unnatural commiserating

nature of weak femininity,
to lead the sanctified family den.
The authoritarian attempt
was to supplant the seeds of justified rejection
toward the bizarre order in youthful minds,
with an astonishing adoration
for the putrid reality,
the acceptance
bearing their own loss of free direction
and the lucid blood
of their superlative inheritance!

Hark!
Oh
ye timeless gods
of high heavens' abode!

I
feel the force of thy anger
at the blasphemous directions
of our sworn leaders,
who continually behave in vain;
who repetitively shake
their repulsive center fingers in thy rigid face,
and enact regulations
that go forthright
in complete opposite direction,
continually assaulting thy sacred consecrations
and repudiating thy precious name!

I
of thee now beseech;
oh ye holy ones on high

deal them all a viscous heavy blow,
cause all of their supporting kingdoms
and inferior adherents to die low
In astonishing heaps!

I
know thy anger is withheld.
I
know that thy mercy is sweet!
But I,
and the all of the Superlative Grand,
shall eternally swear our allegiance
and bow in sacred homage
right now as we all stand,
falling prostrate at thy precious feet!

So
thus allow us,
oh thou heavenly great ones,
to act as thy chosen vessels
of thy enemies' repudiation,
for we greatly desire thy place of redemption
and the restitution
of the former glory
in our cherished lucid blood,
and the divine forthright supremacy
of our exalted Superlative Nation!

We
all bore witness unto
thy ultimate insult,
as they strode before your cherished alter
in baneful masquerade

of that most sacred in holy unions,
all endorsed by the leader
of those gross Moorish infidels,
as he forced his repulsive thumb
into thy angering face!

Your
supreme control
is more evidence
of your superlative glory,
your withholding of all anger shall sustain,
the secret of your future actions lieth
in those most holy of words
that speak so freely of thy
heavenly plain.

The
dark ones know not
of thy future actions,
they know not of their place
or future fate,
for all of them shall grimace
at the forthcoming horrors;
thy consuming fury shall never abate!

Behold
the great conflagration
shall burn for the timeless ages,
their putrid flesh shall provide
an inexhaustible fuel,
then their raging screams
shall betray their present sorrows;
but their time will have

thus,
came into it's conclusion;
their hypocrisy,
their atheism and their blasphemy,
thus,
cannot of time make a loan
or in any way borrow;
for they must now suffer
their consequence
and what by their own choices was
predetermined.

Oh
my heavenly ones. . .,
we long for the opportunity to serve you,
we lust for the chance to redeem thy honor and
give thy supplication for the dark alien order that hath
now been so heavily thrust upon us.

We
desired not that baneful law of the Moors!
We
desireth none of their
scornful repulsive indulgences,
and of their forceful imposing nature
we wish to cause regression,
compelling their complete submission
unto thy perfect law,
holding high only thy golden day!

Please
grant us the precious opportunity
to move forward,

to proceed
according to our divine destination,
to force all their wicked beings
and blighted ones
to simply step aside
from our cherished
anointed command way!

In
perpetual homage
to the glorious among the chosen
I
shall forever maintain my stay,
both in purity of eroding mortal flesh
and
and in the precious sanctity
of superlative eternal
soul sway!

BEHOLD!
In
the rising smoky mist
I bear witness unto the ride of the illustrious
Superlative Grand,
our millions pour forth
from that hallowed castle fortress on high;
like raging floods of water they race across mote
and heavenly gate,
neither time nor wealth can never buy
mercy or repression
of the that which was predestined
to be great!

At
the fore furls
our glorious banner
of the cherished midnight sun,
that all powerful emblem
which shall forever summons
those divinely translucent forces,
that shall evermore stand
until that most appointed task be done!

In
the four directions
go the mighty flood of arms,
born to conquer in according
to those superlative dreams;
all opposing mortals shall flee before them
with great alarm,
all of their ill blood
shall perish in those deep flowing streams!

The
terror of their intrepid thunder
rides upon the distant midday air;
forth from the great woodlands
rise huge flocks of those angelic ravens,
from the grasslands bolt
the hart and the timid hare.
Those
beasts race forward
bearing ominous tidings
unto all those wise enough to seek their council,
but
few mortal shall acknowledge the spirits,

from even the most sanctified of knowledge
they shall forbear!

On
the distant deep
sapphire seas the tempest raged,
and of the sanctified spiritual forces
the island beasts did rightfully adhere,
even the most brutal among men did swear
by the example of the beasts,
and of their lives
they were to give due repair.

But
the wise men of earth
never perceived the obvious knowledge,
and
of that which was divine
they held no care,
so thus,
when the mountains of dark water prevailed,
some five hundred thousand souls,
of their mortal lives
did they eternally forbear.

Even
on the very wind,
my senses perceive the march
of the Magnificent Superlative Grand!
My feet
feel the glory
of their surging thunder
across this divinely allotted land!

The
beasts scamper forward
from their incessant approach,
though it may now be from afar;
in the sacred distance
the rolling evening thunder speaks
of their nearing presence,
with no force on green earth
bearing the capacity to reproach!

Oh
ye superlative men
of mortal earth. . . . .,
Hail
and thus give all glory
unto the Divine Magnificent!
For
in it's reign
thy celestial future advancement
shall
inherit it's marvelous eternal berth!

Those
ancient ghosts
of divine battle beseech me,
my timid ears detect the sweet song
of their precious call,
their urgency pushes our adherents
far out into earth and sea.

BEHOLD,
into the expansive abyss
shall the repulsive scourge of humanity fall!

The
conquering masses
are drawn by the perpetual magnate
of thy faultless life spring,
the revolting man-beasts
shall melt into putrid waste
before our glorious flaming advance,
releasing all emerald earth from the vice
of their clawing grasp;
thence the children of the Superlative
in the voices of angels shall sing,
for now their consecrated future is sealed
into all forward eternity,
their precious destiny to achieve
is finally released;
their illustrious ambition
is like the gracious eagles on the wing,
their extraordinary talents
now are like time infinity,
the precious wealth now of
both heaven and all the earth,
are finally rendered unto their anointed hegemony,
the astonished eyes of their yearning children
at long last
shall behold their ancient patrimony!

With
the might of my arm
and skillful sword,
I lay my enemies asunder;
whilst in the company
of that most magnificent blood
so universally adored,

we shall sweep the boundless fields
of all earth and thus,
shall all of our precious bloods' deceivers
now expunge,
for the nether mortals
shall now all be trampled
thus,
into heaps of infecting dung;
HENCE,
so that we may spread the repulsive mounds
into food for plants
that will ensure
our timeless subsistence.

While
reduced into such capacity
they shall surly bear us no vile potential,
thence only their best positive capacity
via their putrid fleshly supplemental
residue,
rendered only by those redeeming forces
of raging flame,
shall finally justify their base existence
for all those future superlative generations!

Then,
and only then...!
Shall
we illustrious move forward
upon the earth,
into a pristine birth
of superior celestial technological
advancement that will be destined to excel

any that has ever been before
or that shall follow in our wake afterward!

Behold. . ..!
More than nine thousand years ago
into the ancient past,
our superlative fore-bearers
could have certainly attained that most supreme
of desired golden objectives,
but they were weighted down at the ankles
by imposed responsibility unto
those among earths' weak and mentally incompetent.

In fact
much better use of them
could have been made ,
if they could have placed
into coerced service unto those
whom the high command most sought to repress.
Not
only would their use have been better
made in our own interests,
but even made better
in those interests of their own,
since they would have been given specific directions
and the tools needed to
succeed as they traveled along.
Their success would have been guaranteed,
and their product utilized
even into it's greatest
maximum!

Any
wasteful residue
would have utilized
for some determined alternative,
that would have not only benefited the individual people
and those in charge,
but also the entire celestial
earth nation at large!

Our
fore-bearers were very benevolent
with the nether-men of earth,
offering them the very best of schools
bought and paid for by unending funds,
mercilessly extorted
from our superlative majority.

The
vanara-men
did not even bear the responsibility
to perform at an exceptional rate,
since the ruling traitors
from the superlative elites
were well aware
of the vanara-men's inability
to function mentally in the direction
of fore established objective,
the instructors were simply commanded
to re-figure the grades on a scale that would
grant them some seven points to the one,
to counter balance their failing marks.
Those among the superlative
were forced to continue

on their own assumed rate of
outstanding success.

Upon
completing the University study,
the best of employment opportunities
were transferred unto the nether-men of earth.
The vanara-men
were allowed to draw the largest
in gold endowment,
while the superlative were forced to labor
for a fraction of the standard amount;
and the quality of their labor
was then held unto the highest standard,
bearing the subliminal intention
of carrying nether-men dead weight.

From
his seat of employment
the vanara-men could never be removed,
regardless of the degree that he failed to perform
or the funds that his failure cost the corporation.
The
extortion from the superlative
would simply increase
to cover the deficit incurred.

The
vanara-men
were allowed to commit
the vilest of crimes without abate;
Those
among the superlative,

were thus,
prohibited from rushing toward
any weapons take;
if any among the vanara-men
were ever scorned or injured,
then surly the dungeons
or gallows would promptly make
even the greatest among those Superlative Grand,
if placed under the proper pressure,
repent and beg for heavens' pearly gate!

The sin
and wickedness was not allowed
to continue on into an eternity;
soon the currency devalued
and the prices of goods vastly increased,
With much needed commodities
costing more
and the value of the currency increasingly less,
the incessant extortion
was much less in value at it's best.

The gift
of revenue gradually diminished,
the rage of the vanara-men increased
and their unjustified reactions
soon spread into the
elegant neighborhood gates
of those endowed Superlative Grand.
The unjustified rage
of the pergamen were soon to meet
with the cool calculations
of that mighty superlative band!

I
now arise from my toasty berth,
still bearing my body
wrapped tightly in elegant lion skin shirts.

I
grasp my enchanted sword
from my bedside table stand,

I
thus,
seize my dagger blade
from beneath my pillow
and.. . .

I
eternally stride froward
into my proper line of battle..,
forth into dawning infinite life
or my most gruesome death burial hymn,
among those
of the illustrious Superlative Grand!

THE FROGMAN

Many
lands have I,
thus,
roamed..!
My wisdom, skills, and knowledge
has exceptionally grown!
I have known
company to the wisest farmer
and the most ignorant
of the ill informed.
In both woody parks
and city streets
I have beheld
those most intimate
of enlightened deeds,
and those done
within the dreary dark.

AHOY!
I am here
but never perceived,
I am also there
but of my presence
they can never bereave!
I am
a precious delight
in the cheerful wood-side pond,
of those viscous bug plagues
I am very fond!
I can
slumber in the damp shade

for many nights
and days,
but I must forever shun
the most intense of those rays
born from the midday sun.

Aye...
the mid time of night
is certainly my precious delight,
those gentle morsels amble along
and for my take are just right.
None of them ever behold my presence,
I am hidden just as well
in both the dark of night
and in the mid day light!
Though
I speak naught unto the future victims of fate,
the wealth of my knowledge is much more vast
than the mere mortal waste
who only will pledge his allegiance
unto the forces of compulsive task.
Though by most
I am perceived only
to simply lie and wait,
my future actions perceived as unknowable
and my nature to simply hesitate,
I thus await
my magnificent command
to act in play to my part,
for in the style of battle
I am possessed of my own art.

I shall strike

with a certain swiftness
that will both shock the very soul
and destroy the encroaching battle cart!
Behold
I strike from afar
with completely silent air,
at will,
my dreadful titanium dart
passing through both leather
and steel,
the silent haunting poison
to possess the beating of the mortal heart.

Enemy door handles,
tool handles,
and steering wheels,
shall render a menacing numbness
to their touch and feel!

My duties as a warrior
those critics can
thus,
never place in doubt,
just because I lay
all about,
consumed in complete silence,
and
of my presence
I am never known without.

Therefore,
I am certainly one
of the most credible witnesses

unto the insulting horror
that our superlative generations
hath thus endured,
I was
witness unto the great insult
thrust upon them
by their own traitor kindred,
when they subjected their own
to the unchecked whims of the vanara-men,
by promising them freedom
and offering them a false history
of their own supposed pain,
and the wickedness dealt out by those superlative
when
they had been promised a new day
of liberation just the same.

I was
silent witness
unto the unjustified
persecution initiated
by those purloined leaders
of thy sacred promised land.
Thy
illustrious fore-bearer
had spoken the prophetic word,
as we shall all see;
the sacred eternal document
would read
that the wickedness of those possessed
by dark demon of greed,
would surly someday arise in thy sacred
promised land,

to subjugate those now liberated
among the illustrious Superlative Grand!

The
people of emerald earth
would certainly gasp
in astonished surprise!
Where are the patriots,
those mighty men of certain destiny
and
allotted fortune?
Where art thy warrior bands?
Where then,
doeth the cross of blessed
Saint George stand;
the consecrated ring of beaming stars
and golden fire..,
that most splendid marching banner
of the Superlative Grand?

Where
art those heroic
outstanding woodmen?
The
trench bunkers
and their compacted bags
of sand,
those mighty minute men
of glory and
untarnished destiny
in thy graciously allotted land?

Where art thy
cowboys charging forward
on the grassy plains,
their snorting warhorses thundering
ever closer,
the whipping prairie wind
tossing their long mane?

Where
be those steadfast warriors
who stood strong on the Somme,
resisting those forces of tyrannic subjugation
until the last man was gone?

Where
now stands
those awesome warriors
who stood so solidly upon
the golden Norman coast,
that
for generations
their survivors would hoist
that most glorious of toasts,
telling those enthralling tales of valor
and lusty deeds done,
reveling in a mighty warrior's boast!

Wherefore
art those most supreme gallants,
who stood so steadfast to face
the fury of the rising sun,
eternally resisting the looming fear
of death's dark hand,

until that ancient battle for timeless freedom
was won?

I beseech thee,
oh ye valorous men,
avast!
Lend eye
and ear
to the forthcoming command!
For
the approaching
evil lieth not
across the deep blue waters still,
but attack thee
from that most honored
seat of thy own land,
even at it's own will!

The
oppressive alien order
hath thus been thrust
forth upon thy spellbound
boarder;
to dis-regard the absolute evidence
before ye
will lead to future grief,
ye shall then be sold into a vain lie,
left to corrode
in your bewildered disbelief.

Though
multitudes among you
stand

and endlessly complain,
thy jaded complacency forbids ye
to seize thy proper demand,
only to purloin that most anointed liberating gain
from ye issuing generations
and stain
the face of the blessed fore-bearer
who so freely offered thou
the prophetic admonishment.

The
gracious tenth clause
he placed into thy sacred document
for thy eternal preservation.
..alas!

Those
rapacious ones soon sought
only to purloin thou cherished wealth
and entitled extravagance,
most envious of thy unrestrained liberty
and
creative abilities
to service thy own needs outside
of their administrating egoistic domination!

For it was them
who only desired to purloin thou
of thy precious property,
only to force ye into their own
indentured service as it be!

The vile ones
then made catastrophic war
upon the Superlative Grand!
Bearing
the insidious intention
to force their
self serving economic doctrine
throughout
contours of the entire the land!

Through
their alien economic doctrinaire
they continually taint our sacred heir
to unrestrained economic liberty
and wealthy extravagance,
limited only
by the divine regulation of nature
and
the individual skillful imagination
that we all bear!

Behold!
We
are all compelled
to pay those abominable ones
restitution underneath
the guise that they shall serve
our needs best,
but all of us only stand to deny
the very obvious,
when the haunting truth serves
to put our astonished eyes to the test!

The
purloined price
of our restitution only grows
by the month,
whilst our received benefits
only wane in their sickening zest
to disregard our sacred parchment
and the security of liberty therein.

I
behold
the forced removal
of our exalted checks served to crest
the sacred preservation
of our anointed liberty vestibule;
I perceive
many more malicious infringements
that shall surly come.

I
admonish them
as they force our youth
to embrace the abominable sin,
for there they surly tread
upon the most sacred of ground.
In
my holy admonishment
of their diabolical embrace,
shall our certain sanctified restitution
be found!

Behold!
I shall now speak

of what it is that we have to lose..,
they have wrested from us
our precious right to choose!
Does
thou only stand
to disagree with my statement,
does thou still retain the anointed right
to remove thy gifted flesh
from the corrupting company of fools?

Even
though the extortion
serves to provide
an academic improvement,
the immense failure
only continues to prevail throughout
our mandated administrative schools!

Now please consider
thy right to productively engage
in individual enterprise pursuit.....
Whom
is the imposing master
of thy enterprising engagement?
Unto
whom must ye
first make thy solicitation
in appeal to their subjective rule?

Into
whence does
thy labored profit only flow,
into the hand of whom

doeth the fruits of thy labor go?
In lieu
of the twisted extortion
ye should all consequently know
unto whom doeth the supposed benefits bestow?

I
behold
the barbarian invaders,
that by the millions inundate,
and who are allowed to partake
of our purloined healing endowments
until our coffers simply dry up
and break!

The
imposed nether mortal
magistrate
simply serves
to issue the dark mandate,
that we are compelled to support
their limitless hoards
with the very fruits of our labor
and the sweat of our brow,
in lieu of the fiendish order
made in direct cherished reprobate!

Within
the sacred parchment
our admonishing fore- bearer
hath issued that
most cherished of oracles,
fore shadowing our certain future loss of liberty

and our freedom from tyranny gained;
that final check being a celestial access
to both fire and arms,
insuring the might of the people
who should stand
in overwhelming majority against any infringement
of that honored liberating attainment,
even in the very face of death
and eternal destruction
of all that precedes the alarm,
to deny those forces the ability to subjugate
and incarcerate the individual people
for the purpose
of serving only the few
to their own detriment.

Behold!
The wicked one
hath made his presence
among us known!
For he hath sought to deny us
our sworn natural right to liberating arms,
the infecting disease among our intellectual elites
he hath so effectively sown,
based solely on the notion of
an appeal to emotion
appearing justifiable in a public alarm,
by withholding any truth
as it applies unto the villains
whose criminal wickedness he pretends
to reduce!

Were
they not followers of the
negative supreme superlative one?
Did not
their minds fall into the captivating trance
by those bewitching herbs induced,
their ears
thus heard the dark commands
from that wicked son!

The
alien leadership is greatly amused
in their insidious ability to seduce
even our most educated scholars,
thus
has our gifted majority
been effectively won!

Behold
oh ye honorable men
of emerald earth!
Lest we shall dutifully organize
and debate
proper strategic action
and secure our new redeeming berth,
we shall forever lose our blessed lucidity in blood
and liberty at an alarming rate,
and upon our withered necks
will be placed
those insidious jack boots;
we then
shall forever live
only to serve

our sadistic narcissistic masters,
. . ..forsooth!

My duty,
thence,
is to provide a haunting defense,
in the name of liberty
I am to stand against
any outstanding oppressor,
to spread the word unto my fellow men at arms
for my collaborating countrymen
to make that most compelling alarm. . . . .

To arms,
to arms,
in the name of liberty!
In the eternal
name of all that is inherently free!
Race forward,
oh thou superlative ones,
to merge with the magnificent nine mil,
to make holy war with nether mortals
and the vanara-men,
who will only eternally seek to subject us
to their grinding abuse
and then still
will only serve to purloin our precious anointed wealth,
liberty and land again!

Behold
me as I don the secret
warriors special skin.
Spread the word

among our cherished kindred
that ye hath bore witness
as I slip on the honored face.
Tell those warriors tales
as thee behold me slinging
the life giving container
upon my ridged back!

With
the silence of a woodland sprite,
I now ease into the amber waters
of these misty wood.

They
will never notice me as I swim
the watery miles here in the silent midnight wood,
only to surface in places where I can enact
the greatest margin of damage
as any other warrior could!

Aye,
on numerous occasions I can exact
ten times the destruction of the
average fighting man,
both on the land or in
deep blue sea,
or even in fresh water bay;
I have been known to slay hundreds
in the course of a single day!

Just enough
like me out in the world alone
will surly liquidate the nether mortals,

so many do say,
just to put simple figures into
the mathematical equation,
by the way!

If
I should decide to move by sea,
underneath their ships
I can silently go
indeed,
and none of them will ever know!
My breathing bubbles
upon the shifting surface
can thus be carefully contained,
and woe be unto any whom should try
and determine my place!

Underneath
the ships daunting hull
I shall silently swim,
placing that well sealed bowl
into the weakest portion of the keel,
so
that my laboring efforts in thy illustrious service
may
arrive at the most spectacular conclusion
of the day!

THE ARCHER

Behold
all ye valorous men of
good green earth;
I am the archer and please do know
that I have been so since birth!
Both the lion and the jackal have I
dared to hunt,
forever brave in any courageous stunt
with the bow,
sling or fighting staff!

Yes
I have pledged my services to the
blessed march of the nine mil.
I shall complete my duty to the fulfillment
of celestial will.

The
Greeks of old hath given us the
proper story told.
Of
humanities' five levels
did they not speak
during those distant days
when adventure was bold?

Was
not the first level
consisting of the *gold*,
who were the original superlative
so we are told;

the only weakness that they had
was their vice of debauchery,
which in time
proved to be really bad!

The
nether mortals
then had already encroached upon
the magnificent sacred earth,
to purloin superlative wealth
and pollute
with their filthy dirt.

The
transcendent gold then submitted
unto their base weakness
of old,
only to breed with the nether mortals
in the dust,
gratifying their perverted
lusts,
producing offspring without any thought
or care;
until their lusts
and the offensive offspring consumed
all blood,
and from their brilliant kindred
heir,
the emerald earth was soon thus,
bare.

The
superlative gold thus

did silver make,
just as strong in body,
for times sake,
but much less so in mind.
With lower forms of nether mortals
did they breed without
any refrain or care,
nor any sort of precaution take,
until from their kind
the good green earth was bare.

The
new descendants
were those of *bronze*,
more even less in mind,
which was inherent to their kind;
but still they retained strength of body
without repair,
so their diluted blood continued
on without wear.

They descended
on down into the realm of
iron,
where only a superlative few
bore any intellectual mind,
but just as the nether-men beasts,
their bodies were well muscled
and fine.

The
deterioration continues until
this very day,

with the breadth of humanity mixed
with the strength of
iron
in both the body and
intellectual weakness of
clay.

Behold
All of ye anxious men,
for that joyful day shall surly come,
just as the dreary night shall transform into
tomorrows brilliant sun!

For
the sulking clouds shall
surly part,
and that most brilliant
sun shall burn,
when the glorious Superlative Grand
shall make their jubilant return!

Many
straight lines have I thus walked,
and curbs have I taken.
I stand true to my pledge
and shall never think to forsaken,
and of great glory have I to tale!

I was
there when the Spartans
of the glorious three hundred,
did half a million Persians fell,
for the narrow pass of Thermopylae
served us very well.

When
the magnificent King Wallace
stared the glaring British down,
I never once balked!
Have I another great legend here
to tell,
for old Long Shanks simply laid
down his weapons
and walked!

I was
there on the Somme
when more than a million fell,
the allies held their cherished bloodied ground so steadfast,
I know that story all too well!

When
the blitzkrieg came
roaring into the Continent,
it's endless death,
flame and bloody harm that it meant,
I rode with the victorious
in the sacred homeland's defense!

Many
duels and individual situations,
yes I have known my share,
trials and tribulations
have I thus had to bear.

May
all the world know

that now in this glorious fight,
I shall never turn
or give into fearful flight!
Only to stand and do holy battle
doeth give warrior's valor boast;
unto my spirit in the future,
may all my
children give sacred toast!

For it is on
this present glorious day
that the widening sky hath thus opened,
behold the magnificent Superlative hath returned
to claim their precious chosen!

Like
a solid stone wall
in glorious battle,
we Supreme Superlative shall make our brilliant stand,
until we redeem our treasured wealth
and repossess our promised land!

Before
our forward advance
the nether mortals shall melt
with our every heated battle thrust,
until they shall simply just drain away for all eternity
into dirt and dust!

Hence forth
I shall ride to take my battle place
thus,
to forward march with the Supreme Superlative

without regret or fuss.
For behold unto all,
the day of the glorious nine mil hath instantly arrived,
for now their floods pour forth,
I say the exhilarating feelings can never be described!
Forth from the castle mote
we all do boldly ride,
pouring forward throughout the earth,
bearing our unerring allegiance to the ancient heavenly prophesy,
we all must surly abide!

My story here today
thus
have I to tell,
my skill with bow and staff,
shall surly serve thy efforts well.
For some
three hundred yards out,
I hath trained for skill and accuracy make.
Until in complete silence
beneath a helmets edge,
in a single eye
can a life my arrow take.

Into the air
go bags of straw,
I shall fill them full with my arrows
before the fall!
The hoop shall roll upon the grass
of the meadow wood,
all my arrows fly strait
and true,
into the very center as they should.

In yon field
stands those man sized silhouettes
looming like wicked brigands
moving forward to rob,
rape,
pillage
and make sooty waste,
into both forehead
and heart go my arrows,
straight
where they command,
in absence of withholding conjecture
or haste.

With
great wager in gold
in contest
do I casually make,
I have as yet
to return without gain
or in sadness my nourishment take!

My skill
hath delighted both King
and woodmen as it may,
for I won
the hand of the gentle maiden,
and she unto my heart
did wed
for my better sake.

In the kings' name
I chose to duel,

guaranteeing that no harm
shall come his way,
preserving all truth in his word
since I always bore the final say!

In the King's name
I hunt both boar and hart,
supplying his table with luscious nourishment
still,
both sweet and tart,
patrolling his wood to eliminate
the thieves with the skill
in my blessed art!

I hath
been so divinely commissioned
to patrol the Lords property,
giving complete comfort in his security
and insuring his property rights.
I am contented
to simply make my rounds
in the brilliance of day,
or the dim lights
of the darkest nights!

As of yet
I have never miss-stepped,
and for my endeavors
I have always come through;
I accredit this
with those genetic gifts
of the Superlative too!

Unto the entire emerald earth
have I a duty to contemplate,
for the advancing future of all mankind
can simply just not wait.
The dreadful weight upon their ankles
hath caused all gifted to forbear
the fruits of all their laboring efforts
and those of their innocent heirs;
thus,
in the name of economic liberty
shall I ride forward
and swear
with all my might
to sacrifice
all of the present
into the glorious fight;
yea thus,
all knowing that the exalted conclusion
shall be to our
jubilant delight!

So ride
do so boldly ride,
ye victorious among the nine mil!
Ride for virtue,
honor and glory,
and thy superlative redemption still!

THE HIGH PRIESTESS

T hy cherished name,
Lavenna,
speaks so boldly of thy sacred skill,
to communicate both with those spirits neigh
and the immaculate Adonis on high,
on any moment of thy chosen will.

That most grand of temples
is to be here on earth blissfully bestowed
as thy mortal coveted heavenly abode,
for it is by thy call that immaculate Adonis
shall make known unto all,
that most precious moment of the mighty warriors' mode!

From the most humble
of beginnings ye were chosen best,
both delicate in body
and humble in manners,
moderate in ailment
and dress.

Forward from the plains of Taura
thou didst humbly hail,
body firm in dutiful labor,
mind soaked
in the cherished knowledge well.

Ye was tutored in the arts of the battle staff,
skill with sword
and dagger hath

preserved thee into thy sanctified knowledge,
they tell.

Thy mentor was
the distinguished magician,
Ozzymoddor,
deep down in ancient castle lair
didst thee dare to venture,
to learn those mysterious dark traditions
whist in his gracious indenture.

Behold,
ye didst learn
to mix exotic herb and spice,
those unseen spirits in thy chamber
didst thee entice.
Beseeching those appeals
for future knowledge yet unknown,
never aware of those dark seeds
that thee may be a sowing.

But didst thee
learn thy secret talents very well,
my dear Lavenna,
for that yearning Angel,
Bran The Blessed,
didst appear
and giveth thee meaning
unto those majestic songs
that *Ozzymoddor* kept on a singing.

So it was said
that above a deep stone fissure

didst thy hold thou enlightened head. . .
Thus
forward into somber trance
didst thy soul dare to go;
on thy pillow whilst thee lay in silent slumber
did the ghost seek for thee to play
and all that thee could do
was just to simply fear
in dreadful dismay;
for matters would have been so much better,
so it hath been jestingly said,
if thee could only just slumber quietly
in thy nice warm bed!

But thy true lesson
in thy experience was for thee
to simply behold
and respect those
from which thy knowledge
had came to stay!
For the dark lesson
that thee must learn
is that in those haunting ghosts,
the immaculate Adonis
could appear unto his adoring hosts,
and then by directly speaking his words
he could,
alas,
make his will
eternally known.

It was thou
who heard thy holy call

from the tersea sable sun
there in the midst of thy vast courtyard floor.
Thus the warrior multitudes
didst assemble,
those well trained lancers
and swordsmen
were extremely nimble,
as thy masses took their place
before the immense courtyard archway door.

In the midst
of thy midnight slumber
didst the Adonis recite his orders for
those grand proceedings
in the colossal mansion assembly yard.
When the prophet
took his pedestal place
before the all attentive masses,
and the illustrious emperor
glared down into those
yearning faces hard,
he spoke the words revealed in thy precious meeting
born from those spirits that thee was seeking,
and hence,
the commanding words
from the mighty Adonis
could thus be spoken.

Behold,
our vows unto the superior emerald earth
can never be broken!
It is our calling
and our holy endeavor to take

the treasured gift from
those inferior
and non deserving,
that so wickedly scheme to make
the wealth of all our divinely allotted promised land
as their sole token!

Tremble in thy boots,
oh ye wretched inferiors!
Thee can never purloin
that gracious inheritance
that was sublimely bestowed;
now is the day
that all of ye shall so astonishingly learn
that the Divine Magnificent Genetic Superlative
hath hence forth forever returned!
Forth from the earth into our bliss,
thy tainted blood shall be scorned by all
in thy well earned blame. . .,
Those who dare to question
then do know this. . . . .,
it shall be purged away for ever
by both sword and flame!

Behold!
I hath pledged my very life
unto the mighty wave
from the anointed land,
that superlative army of the Divine Magnificent Grand!
It will be upon our sanctified shores
that I shall make my eternal stand,
only to live and die
in my hallowed heartland.

Today I shall ascend into my majestic abode,
to anticipate the divine call from my immaculate Adonis
and
only tp contemplate the proper chant and spell,
to study the clandestine charms
and the herbal mixtures well,
only to hear dreary words faintly spoken
from those scheming poltergeist abroad,
offering their occultist instructions
for those anointed advancing warriors marching
proudly in perpetual row
from thy mansion courtyard hall.

Behold!
Their most magnificent leaders
all cometh unto me
for encouragement
and future knowledge gained
from those most
divine ghosts indeed!

I am the honored mediator!
Without my efforts there will be no majestic advance.
There will be no foresight that allows us
to anticipate the enemies' next abhorrent moves.
Without this divine anticipation,
then the weaknesses
of the advancing opposition may never be
deduced!

On the ground observation
certainly has it's due place,
but the ability to anticipate actions unknown

in the make,
combining this dawning exhilaration
with knowledge gained by our roaming scouts,
both efforts merging to ensure our solid victory
within and without!

Know this in as much,
all ye among the superlative of green earth,
my temple stands grand bearing
three hundred steps up
toward the most elaborate artistic elegance
as such.

The front door
enshrouded in a crimson dragon's tail
as an
enveloping vine,
inside a softly swinging pendulum keeps rhythmic time,
casting forth misty spells unto those spirits
most sublime.

Inside
upon the sable sun emblem
on the floor,
I shall alight the twelve golden candle sticks
for those
commanding superlative generals to adore,
to sing the sacred chants aloud
whilst we stand about so ridged and proud!

In minutes
the sacred mood shall transform,
and our eyes

shall behold that astonishing misty cloud,
and then our ears will behold
those heavenly voices as they scorn
our enemies
and give praise unto our conquering intentions.
Soon they all
shall so majestically appear,
their shimmering reverberations
by our side so near.

One by one
I shall indeed make record of their noble form. . ..
Behold
those majestic gods
of the Divine Magnificent Superlative
now reborn!

Forth
from the damp mists
of those most distant enchanting times:

Admire
divine *Lugus,*
both mighty and bold,
offering unto us his gifts of knowledge
and wisdom in battle untold.
Through his sacred guidance
and precious insight,
with our consistent valor
and success,
we shall certainly vanquish the
filthy nether mortals
in the forthcoming glorious fight,

stomping them all into dung with our cherished
superlative best!

Witness thy honored
Belanus,
standing before us straight and true.
He shall
be the one to heal
our battle wounded
with the astonishingly gracious power
that he will use!

Now entereth the immaculate
Tridiamous,
just his mere presence commands
all of our respect.
For it is by his power
and gracious virtue
that we shall have abundance
and inherit our astonishing success!

Into the dazzling front
we shall initiate our mighty test,
so shall the divine
Taranis
first bring great thunder
from the enemies' daunting west!

Now will follow our appeal to
Boryum,
who shall engage the howling winds
with great zeal,
to force the entire army

of the villains
to bidden for mercy
and kneel;
for thus
they may remain prostrate,
submitting only unto our commanding will.

Now shall rage the terrible
Arausio,
who shall causeth all
consuming liquid volumes
to flow,
possibly washing away
the tainted villains
into the deepest depths
of raging purgatory,
we shall all hope!

At long last
we will be obliged
then to make our grand appeal
unto the supreme
Cicolluis
who shall allow our mighty army
to passionately
proceed without resistance;
our abhorrent opponents melting still,
submitting only
unto our imposing superlative inclination,
granting us our long house boasting rights
by providing us our constant thrill!

So completely
submerged into thy absolute service
I do solemnly commend myself,
my sacred knowledge
and my coveted skill;
likewise I commit all of my golden wealth,
my innate passions
and my will.
Amid thy dazzling
wake across all the emerald earth,
I shall with my own knowledge
and presence
enhance thy victorious berth,
if only just to partake in the exhilarating thrill,
until our imposing enemies stand forever nil,
now the eternally silenced victims
of their own anointed curse!

One by one
the gods are aligned,
all eternally craving for the enemies' worst;
all standing proudly poised
and ready to offer the commandment
for us to storm ahead
in our most triumphant burst!

THE LOVERS

Observe
our presence among thine own..,
those most enduring blissful of moments
that indeed have we enjoyed,
only to neutralize the frustration
and pain that we have known.
For the merry thrill of new adventure
we shall boldly employ,
only to relinquish any wrenching anger
that was previously sown
by this opposing abuse dealt out by the nether mortals
that we simply could not ignore.

So both to
avenge the desecration of our sacred land
and for the merry thrills. . .,
we shall now boldly ride!
Submitting only
to the precious Adonis' radiating will,
trusting the wisdom of superlative gods,
the perfect skill of those sacred magicians
and the diviners to abide
with the truth,
offering us only proper forthcoming instruction
to be blessed still
by that most adorable Adonis on high!

First
from the emerald plains of Eire
we made our hail,
taking our abode among fair maidens

and the loving pixie sprite;
of thy secret knowledge
we learned our share very well,
commencing to function
in both the bright
of day or the moon
of night.

We mixed thy herbal potions,
we prayed thy haunting chant,
we then received our enrapturing instructions
and increased our golden might.,
then from each and every possible adventure
we could never recant!

Forth onto many distant sands
we have made our happy abode,
moving only where the feeling has led us
and we could easily purchase land.
In each and every place
our eyes did behold a solemn truth,
though
no matter how much it was that we tried to ignore it,
it's demonic grasp did expand!

The
nether mortals hold the blessed emerald earth
in their approaching clutches,
do know !

For
it was our graciously anointed endowment,
this entire sacred land!

For it is
among those crimson roses
and sweet lavender wisteria arbor
that we both
stood to make our spiritual pact and
where we made our vows,
placing the exalted band upon our trembling fingers,
promising only to adore each other
until the seas cease in their rhythmic serge
into golden sand,
only to follow one another until
our deaths due make us part.

We shall travel
forward into our lives' adventure,
forsaking all other women or man,
for we hath taken our honorable pledge
from both the mind and yearning heart.
We chant in unison it is until death that by each others blessed side
we shall make our altruistic stand!

So forth as
shines our pledge unto one another,
so shall we incessantly commit our selves
unto the sacred cause
of those Superlative Grand,
waging war unto the very end,
until the venara-men are stomped asunder,
living to behold that most glorious day when
we all shall radiate in brilliant glory!

Into the
surrounding universe

bearing our illustrious wealth
and creative wonder,
all shining for eternity
underneath a glowing brilliant sun,
like the perfect ending in an ancient fairy tale story.

Our love shall
thus,
play it's chosen part,
to spread our own kindred across
this graciously anointed land
that we hath so valiantly won.
From that very moment forth
we doeth know our great command,
which is to encourage the same
among our own daughters and sons!

Our future duty
for the precious cause
is outstanding in it's design and scope,
but for the enduring superlative nothing less
shall be accepted in labor or fun.
A supreme empire
shall arise from the emerald land,
it's dazzling magnitude alone shall
offer forth-ward thy everlasting hope.

Within it's illustrious center shall stand
the emerald temple of
Adonis The Grand,
then the palace courtyards
and cottages of all the people thereabout
shall stand in eternal glory throughout the entire land!

All of our people
shall then
dwell in eternal extravagance indeed,
the blessed intent of the holy Adonis and
the superlative God of all Gods,
Ahuramazda. . ..,
and then his son shall unto earth return
to walk among the oaks
and luscious flowering pods,
offering his everlasting salvation unto his chosen volk.

Lend ear all thy universe,
then the anointed task shall be complete,
Behold,
the fairies and angels
shall become our worshiping nurse!

Those glorious hymns
of illuminating praise
we shall thus sing all throughout,
giving eternal praise unto the blessed son,
Zorothrausi;
for the genetic inferiors
of all the earth
thus,
will then have known
the horrors of his dreadful damning curse!

Unto
the high priestess
we once did make our solemn employ,
laboring to stir the potions and chant the seducing charms,
conjuring those enlightened spirits

and specters of those long dead alter boys;
to give us the blessed instructions
and to sound the proper meditating alarms
all about,
to those high leaders in the enchanted hallways
. . .at least;
then we would give refined lecture
unto the massive body of listless
people without.

From here
it was that we learned
thy sacred wisdom well
and the most ancient history of the earth,
so thus,
the story of earth
and man doeth we have thee to tell.

It was in a time of dense fog
and gray mist that all life had it's birth,
for the ancient seas covered all
from mountain unto grassy meadow dale;
the proof in those words today
is from the many shells
that children find on high berth.

From the very beginning
there was nothing,
thus
but the seas and the expansive azure globe. . .
But the mighty
Ahuramazda
moved all about

to cover the face of the deep,
and he then strove
to initiate the arrival of time
and the beginning of life throughout.

He spoke the thundering words
into the timeless heavenly abode,
and the clouds parted to expose
a glowing radiance,
that without a doubt,
dried the sulking mist
and the fog
to establish a much more pleasant mode;
and the forces of those cheerful rays
then caused the raging waters to recede;
when the entire earth violently shook,
causing the land underneath
to break far below,
for the new land did then arise upward
from the murky bottom of the sea.

"Behold. . ..!"
The great
Ahuramazda then said;
"All is well with this wonderful new exposure,
so hence forth the emerald earth
shall be thy eternal bed!"

Thus did the plants grow
into a verdant blanket that was really kosher;
so the great Ahuramazda then said,

"Let new life
now unto the emerald earth be wed!"

Soon did all beasts,
both great and small,
fill the entire planetary enclosure
as indeed it surly should,
and thus did
Ahuramazda gaze forward
and sayeth aloud;

"All that now
stands before me
is pleasant to see and good;
Lets do place man
into the canopy to roam among the beasts
and be led
by the power in my voice
and the wisdom in my words
as they would."

Down from the heavenly skies
came those most majestic beings,
who established their own illustrious kingdom
within the emerald canopy
bearing their elegant superlative good!
Soon the mighty expanses did sing
with the hammering ringings
from the massive construction of elaborate temples
that stood
within the shade of the emerald canopy,
inviting those tidings
from the wealthiest clans. . .,

possessing a crucial part
was a strong desire for supreme success
from every majestic man.

In what seemed like a blink,
the verdant earth was alive with the illustrious kingdom
and their crying new births..
But soon the dark lord
of the negative superlative
gazed forward and became jealous;
he mixed the secret herbs
and chanted a spell bearing a damning curse,
causing the very elements
within the earth
to attack the superlative with a raging zeal,
poisoning their blood with mutating genes
so that many would only experience the worst,
inducing the blessed superlative to eventually submit
unto his negative will,
since the majority had lost their ability
to reason and deduce his wicked curse!
That dark Lord of the negative superlative
then let lose with another damning burst. . ..!

So the grand
kingdom was destined to excel
standing strong and tall for some three thousand years,
our generations have listened well;
but then when it was least to be expected
the unthinkable did happen in time
as they tell;

Among the beasts
did suddenly come to exist
a base humanoid kind,
who scrubbed with the wild herds
and the rancid swine.

He subsisted mainly upon roots,
various grains and herbs,
but only hunted meat
when the motivating desire did compel.

Though the females
were never very attractive
in any entrancing way,
the only weaknesses in the superlative
was the desire for their enticing favors,
we hear tale;
so thus,
by both the light of day
and the moon of night
they were very active,
by the creek bank,
by rushing river and dale,
behind the bushes very frequently they fell!

The years passed by
on that superlative grand and
their true kind did soon pass from the earth,
so the elders do tell,
and the supposed beauty from the mixed young
did now prevail across the land,
for the perverse weakness of debauchery
did serve to eradicate very well!

But on
one starlit night
the great
Ahuramazda
did send forth his glorious son as a simple babe,
bearing the single purpose of delivering the very best in man
on a future magnificent date!
He declared that
the original genetic superlative
he would both redeem and save,
the only task for mankind to achieve
is too remain genetically chaste
and to simply wait!

When it is that he shall return
no one knows not,
it could be on a cheerful Friday or
on a blustery Wednesday in a trot.
I would prefer
a timeless Tuesday
just in case we have forgot;
but certainly his name
shall stand for all intrinsic eternity.,
Behold the invincible
Zorothrausi!

THE CHARIOT

Cometh hither thy blessed cart,
thy plaustrum of the patronizing gods!
Endowed with the glitter from the angels on high,
blessed with the power of the birds in flight,
it shall be you who is destined to carry the supreme
into eternal victory!

Forth from the heights of the skies ye shall race,
through those vast expanses of time and boundless void of outer space.
Again ye shall demonstrate thy blessings first,
when ye shall race across the ragged landscape
in a massive triumphant burst!
Delivering fire and terror into thy enemy's face,
sending them headlong for all eternity into their proper place.

In the distance my ears do cheerfully perceive
thy thundering advance across the looming earth praeter.
My exhilarated heart doeth hammer at the thought
of thy celestial acquisition,
of all earth, much of space, land and sea,
hail to the thought of our blessed blood
being reestablished into it's anointed position!

It was from him that thy generous blessings came,
so shout his blessed name with glee,
for it is through him that our blood
is relinquished of all tarnish and blame;
shout Hail unto
Zorothrausi!
Hail unto the great
Zorothrausi!

So

shall the stars in heaven sing our glorious victory song,
for the power is reassigned unto those whom it justly belonged.
The entire earth shall sing of our superlative glory and might,
the resurrected lucidity of our coveted blood retained,
the creative magnitude of our dazzling temples and lights!

For it was through us that all culture and elegance reigned,
but naught just hath not been the same
since we were forced to merge into that most base of debauchery
bearing nether-man blame!
Into great poverty and want the earth did thus descend,
but for thousands of years we cried unto you to make immaculate amends!

So on this glorious day didst thou call
that mighty superlative army forth,
to move upon the mortals of a rancid dying earth,
offering precious deliverance
and the wonder of new glorious birth;
to purge the wicked taint
from our perfect superlative blood,
with the heat of intense white flame,
swift sword of lightening and flood!

Of perfect gold be thy precious material make,
studded emeralds along thy slanting sides,
for the ultimate glory thy staggering impression take.
Into the direction of thy enchanting captains' guide
shall we rush headlong into thy furious wake.
Devoted solely unto that gleaming goal at steak,
unto that cherished route thy driver shall eternally abide!

That most precious gift unto all mortal earth
shall there timelessly thrive,
rising upward into a glorious height,
resurrecting a technologically advanced society
that simply can no longer wait.
Those that thrive can ride that colossal swelling wave
without anxiety or haste,
sealing their place among the superlative
gifted forward from this very date.

Our illustrious kingdom that we have strove to raise
canst never be allowed to be consumed by vermin and worms,
wresting our precious glory and magnitude from all that we design to amaze.
Was it not our predestined way to reign from our superlative place and concerns,
since we were allowed to arise by that supreme Lord of the Superlative race?
For seventy years that great defining crucible hath been allowed to reign righteously
among those mortals who dwell in descending apathy on emerald earth,
thus they by their own inherited apathetic nature determine their defining place.

See,
those that desire to examine the system at large,
learn,
and properly educate,
shall thus inherit the glorious kingdom charged
with transporting mankind into a new illustrious era
that can no longer be forced to abate.
Thus,
those that inherit the mutated tendency to posses apathy,
academic slothfulness,

and simply refuse to conform or their own instate
with zeal;
will thus determine their forlorn place,
and their own position in the coming consuming furnace
will they only choose to seal,
and by their own choices determine to make.

Unto

thee my gloriously majestic enraptured chariot,
thy powers of propulsion born from our brilliant God
didst thy stand to receive and by constructing repetition inherit,
thus thee were blessed by his eternal superlative nod.
Behold,
it is not unto thee that we stand in submissive worship,
but thy majestic powers invested
by our immortal superlative Lordship and
thy place in his incessant plan.

Like

a brilliant meteor looming in the distant mid-night sky
ye streaked forth superseding all time and space,
racing toward thy programmed goal on high,
all of mortal humanity could only gaze forward
with an astonished prolonged sigh.
Into thy mind was punched thy brilliant destiny
contributing toward that most exhilarating kingdom
being established on planet earth,
neutralizing those nether mortal efforts,
condemning them even before their actions are even berthed!

Behold

the very precedence to thy magnificent arrival upon mortal earth
exist even with this very moment in time and place.

The mortals perceive not of thy forthcoming berth.
Standing consumed in their radiating ignorance to date,
with the suggesting facts looming before them even in their very face!

Fathom ho!
Oh ye apathetic mortals of emerald earth,
the mighty divisive crucible stands even now in thy very midst!
Does thee not comprehend the advancing wisdom that exists,
the reducing value of thy labors worth?
Calculate thy true figures among those labor-less,
those weary ones in desperate plight,
those whom daily are subjected unto constant wantonness. . ..
Count all those whom for looming months on dreary end
are in search of labor and simple opportunity for basic sustenance,
whom are reduced into skipping meals and going sick without mend.
Do count only those true figures of more than fifteen percent,
do deduce those facts that the experts relate claiming those figures will never bend!
The new superlative wisdom is replacing the need for the dutiful services of men,
thus the ranks of the unemployed will soon swell by more than twenty five percent!
In a mere ten year expanse those masses will rise into a figure of thirty five,
in a number of places on earth that figure will rise to more than seventy when
they cry unto the ruling authorities only demanding to know the reason why.
Thus the magisterial authorities will hand out supplemental funds again,
but thy demands upon thy minority source for those supplements
will raise until they are nearly dry.

Why,
they shall scream unto their superlative lord

standing high in the sparkling mid-night sky?
Why should we be punished by our toil and sweat,
when through our gifted efforts that thy blessed
illustrious kingdom on earth cometh neigh?
Force those receiving multitudes to labor,
allow their dripping sweat to make earnest purchase by,
allow their grinding labor to produce for those whom never waver
in their pursuit of grand achievement and glittering prosperity!
Why should the blessed anointed support those whom favor
their bread from charity?

Thus
then shall the elite accomplished few rule with the large majority supporting
ever pressing subsidization to keep them alive,
without any demand that labor be imported
so that they with their own efforts could thrive.
With the course of time did the elite come to resent
those problematic solutions that the authoritarians of earth did buy,
so they determined to rectify their problems for themselves and mend
through their own anointed creativity.
With the great new multiplicity in man-kinds' population and
demand for earths productive resources causing massive poverty and depravity,
it was soon conceived that addressing action needed to be taken
to retain those resources and the land among the ingenious superlative indeed.
The newly adopted religion gave the proper justification
to their creative situation and a new comforting morality
unto their all consuming plans' most direct application!

Behold
those most accomplished were justified by superlative genes,

those ancient heavenly beings blessing them with creative skills and talents to excel!
Inherently the entire earth was theirs by right of superior blood
and their creative wings.
Since their kind controlled the corporations
and all of the government entities and enterprise.
It should then come as no mighty surprise or elation
when they choose to allow their own congregation to dominate
the entire new world nation!

Thus
that elite sought
to reduce the entire majority population
into a mere resource for their own use and wrought
from all of them their laboring best
by being subjected to their ceaseless abuse!
When they had thus extracted their maximum limit,
into the white hot furnace their worn
and ragged bodies would thus be tossed,
and their once soaring populations
consequently reduced into a perishing plummet,
until for them their lives
and all the beauty of emerald earth is permanently lost.

With the precious land of earth and the natural resources now free,
those elites among all mortal men
can advance and pursue to seek the upward rise
in a most illustrious magnificent empire of technological assent.
Across the entire world the fact will most assuredly stand
that their retaining leg weights have now demised;

Hurrah!
presently they are free to advance forward

in their illustrious achievement
without repressive,
despised
bereavement,
and begrudging responsibility.

STRENGTH

is the supreme superlative blessing
for all the lower beings of earth to behold.
Might of arm holds that special charm in it's stand, caressing
that muscled body of the battle hardened and bold;
but the force of both wisdom and gracious wit offers a superior dressing
to the outstanding success of that most supreme endeavor
to advance the earth in those most illustrious directions yet untold!

Might
is the force of all the gods in heavenly domain,
the great engagement that moves mountains
and changes the course of massive flowing rivers,
that defeats armies when exhaustion sets in to retain
the glory of conquest from within the victors' champagne!

Thus
Strength is determined by trial of fire
which purges all negative impurities from both superlative blood
and steel,
and gold,
like strength of character that is purged
by great tribulations and negative floods!
The mighty person is determined
by opposing contests in numbers untold!

Will
is the superlative base for the seed of might
in outstanding character,
and even strength in body still!
Thus
persistence is determined by that superlative base,

will,
which is the fertile ground for an incessant endurance,
with the never ending exposure to adversity fostering
might,
producing that greatest of wonder in both
body and mind,
in conjunction with determined character,
Strength!

Behold,
The great
Zorothrausi
is the epitome of might and persistence!
He motivated the formation of all the earth from nothingness.
From dust of the earth,
fire and the energy within his very breath,
he created precious life.
The original superlative of man descended within the midst of that life,
born from the stars and due to continuing strife,
made their great escape from that planet
where once the wealth of all the universe
was locked.

On earth they were instructed
to tend the precious emerald canopy and
the natural flocks.
By the shear force stored within his voice,
every form of life knew it's place and proper duty stations.
Their bodies became ripped with raw bulging muscles
of brawny might to employ,
their hair ran like threads of pure gold
or curled like crimson locks,
their skin shone extremely fair

and their youth raced about
in perfectly contented jubilation.

Thus. . ..
this splendid majestic world
was created by force of will
and might!
The shear power locked within a single voice actually drove
the impenetrable dark of dreary night into
the radiating glow of a dawning ultramodern day!

Those
greatest among the superlative did possess
one single digress,
deep down into the realm of debauchery
were they so callously given,
thus
the envious lord of the negative
knew where he could press
for the purpose of causing the destruction
of an astounding magnificent creation.

Behold. . .,
he thus did create his own negative creation
but one so bold
that their ape like wenches
walked among those mighty superlative men,
and born within those future unions
was their own genetic destruction to behold.

In truth,
the very elements within the earth itself
had previously been cursed,

first causing the eroding tainted blood,
. . . . .forsooth!

Thus the mutated gene eliminated the wisdom's berth
to refrain from the debauchery with the nether-man harlot that grew
into that most base deterioration of all man-kind!

In this manner
even the slightest lacking of strength
leads into a wholesale destruction of the worst kind!
The most anointed among us should always search
and endeavor
to improve on the majestic quality in both arm and character;
this great endeavor is to continue on for endless infinity,
just as long as mankind exists and is endowed with the cleaver
wit and positive intention to excel.

Strength
will stand eternally to separate the casual curiosity from
infinite dedication,
destined to engender imagined endeavors
into a realm that astounds mortal eyes!
Through dedication stand those magnificent works towering tall
to reign for an immortal manifestation!

Power of strength
eternally transcends into force of will,
that engenders a persistent determination
to see the rightful victor through,
and the steel
of his instructive will placed upon those whom know not
the superlative instinctive direction
of preciously endeavored supreme mortal success.

Only those precious attributes of an outstanding success
should reign forthright,
giving magnificent acknowledgment unto those who stand
nearest unto the supreme superlative original!

Euphemistic lies designed
to elevate the nether-man in the eyes
of youthful beholders can never reign supreme in the face
of timeless facts that are natural,
giving precious honor and justified tribute
unto the superlative brilliance,
thus always,
no matter how the enemy tries,
the supreme truth is always destined
to overshadow base propagandist lies!
 . . . . ..Hence
in the force of honesty
stands the supreme strength and might
of the absolute truth.

The physical manifestations
of the superlative absolute truth
stands to give reinforcement of that illuminating legitimacy
already intrinsically known
all across precious emerald earth.

Behold the immaculate cathedrals
that stand to radiate illumination
to the emerald landscape. . ..!

Take immediate view of those huge
majestic plantation farm estates,
reigning infinitely supreme from a time

when men could rise up by the forces of nature
in complete absence of any repressive tyrannous regulation. . .. . ..!

In thy illustrious museums
stands their astounding delicate art. . ..,
upon thy music sheets plays
that classical enrapturing majestic sound
of superlative endowment and creative imagery. . ..!

By force of might arose thy nation
itself into an outstanding beckoning supremacy,
thy very foundation in enshrined law
exists as a sole manifestation of superlative virtue
and an artistic creative endeavor,
thy precious anointment born from the
original genetic superlative!

Fathom
in thy most developed visionary
those long lost days of ancient creative glory,
and the power of perceptions and originality that has
taken all of us and our beloved
superlative genetic kindred into this dawning
of neo technological ultramodern Elysium. . .!

Perceive
the astounding base for all of this mesmerizing achievement. . . . .!
In the course of thy laboring logic and analytical deduction,
behold the illustrious source of the imaginative creativity and
blessed persistence to pursue the perilous dream
until the very staggering end,
thy base, wretched, corroding worms of emerald earth!

. . . . . . .Strength. . . . . .!
Now through virtue of comprehension
and inhalation of our superlative strength,
behold the vision of our own complete conquest and
the glory of our supreme accomplishments when all the entire emerald earth
is no longer restrained by your own incompetence and
repulsive, nauseating, inability to succeed in
a world that flies far far beyond your genetic
capacity to simply envision. . ..,
most certainly lying far beyond your ability to succeed,
and even lying far beyond your ability to
simply just survive. . . . .!

Tell me. . ..,
oh ye repulsive, leaching, coprophagous worms,
why should
our obligated duty be to provide ye with thy daily subsistence,
why should not the primeval law
of natural selection then reign
supreme?

The earth would certainly be far less congested and
much more productive without thy consuming decadence and
pathetic wanton waste..!
Then thy repulsive squalor and contamination could be
eternally replaced by lavish wealth and luxuriant accomplished
productivity.
Thy arecaceae enshrouded wastelands converted into majestic fields of
date palms,
calculatingly placed among luscious agave and the glory of the mango
pine apples.
Then this outstandingly productive agriculture
strategically graced by our gloriously majestic colonial

mansions,
flying high the immortal flag of Saint George
in their welcoming promenade,
housing thousands upon precious thousands
of those who are most deserving of the climate and the
extravagant wealth..!

Pause now
for just a single moment and ponder,
all of the above in it's conception has sprung from it's single,
most forcefully dominant base,
STRENGTH!

SANCTIUM MUNERA IN DONARIIS

By brilliance of our colossal uniting bonfire
we shall stand strong on the plaga duodecium
in sacred unison to take our consecrated vow!
Before us stands tall the flaming cross of good Saint Andrews,
immortally consecrated in the blood of freedoms' spirit
and the gray ghost of our long lost fortitude.

Forward from the radiating warmth of our hearths
we march to the spiritual call of duty,
bearing the blessed intent of massive transformation in the name
our precious purloined heritage and constitutional liberty.

In mighty spiritual and physical unison,
we among the glorious nine mil,
raise our right hands forward toward
the flaming cross in the forbidden Bellamy salute,
absorbing the resurrected spirit of freedom
and the ancient gray ghost of our resuscitating fortitude!

Inside we all behold the comforting warmth
of our new spiritual possession.
In outstanding declaration
we feel massive swelling jubilation
at our emerging sense of duty and obligation!

We, among the blessed nine mil, have sacrificed all in the name
of our looming precious resurrected liberty.
By our hearths sit our patient wives,
bearing our sons and daughters wrapped
in the swaddling clothes of our individualist endeavors and intention. . .,
the very life's' blood of altruistic sacrifice

and the immortal embrace of constitutional liberty at
the complete expense of repressive tyranny in it's every future form.

Behold,
it is with them
that the incessant motivation
for the realization of our outstanding call
to arms and altruistic liberty came,
blaring loudest into our lusting ears and hearts yearning for
the thrill of action at it's greatest level of intensity,
followed by the thrill of our massive victory jubilee celebration!

Presently our masses only sit in great anticipation
of the forthcoming conclusion,
many thousands only languishing deep inside
of our fore-constructed tunnel bunkers,
the bunker basements of homes that have been shattered,
forming colossal heaps of rubble that both conceal and effectively protect.
Let even their names stand in radiant eternal glory
for the warriors that they are,
in the honor of timeless liberty
and an altruistic gift of service to the great supreme cause!

In our superlative genius
we have deduced the necessity
of developing concealed manufacturing facilities in presumption,
most existing as a part in a bunker system within themselves,
some standing by themselves with only those bunkers for the workers,
whom are certainly true superlative warriors in their own right.

Our grand efforts at the production of victual subsistence
we have deduced in our presumptive figures as well.
Most importantly,

however,
we have supported these deductions with an ever essential
plan of action.
By use of our superlative engineers
we have so effectively designed our appropriate plans,
that we have astounded the world of our mortal inferiors with our workmanship
and developed imagination.

Behold,
we were all once only as average mortals whom
only existed among common earthlings,
but
median beings who were restrained by repressive neo-Marxist regulation,
instituted underneath the guise of restitution
for some sort of fantastic wrong wrought in the ancient past
by our superlative fore-bearers,
upon those who
would otherwise bear no direction born by their own self guiding deduction
and imagination.

In reality
this repressive regulation was the true wrong,
and this regulation was forced upon all in complete absence
of their personal majority endorsement.
Even those of whom were in reception of the restitution,
were in fact,
unknowing victims of their own indemnity!

Thus,
their inability to perceive their own shackles,
preferring to accept the lie that they were being properly rectified,

only stands to serve the conclusion of their being in possession of genetic mutation that prevents logical deduction.
This reality also
stands to confirm that even those within their own government
perceived them only as fools ripe for their own exploitation.!

Imagine that.,
a filthy debauched belligerent slave bearing
outstanding insolence and radiating forth only a base pathetic ignorance,
whom is actually convinced,
even to the very point of raging violence and self sacrifice,
that he is free
due to a mythologized "sacred preordained" parchment declaration!

We among the superlative
strong and eternally brave,
towering forever in reverberating admonishment of that tainted,
now tarnished claim,
that we are free!
We take direct action and make the supreme sacrifice based on conclusion
of intelligent presumptive deduction and analytical reasoning,
that we among the superlative and all otherwise,
are resoundingly *NOT* free!
We base our sanctified plan of action out of this deductive reasoning
in now obvious conclusion..,
hence,
by our movement into action we have simultaneously
established our material and emotional sacrifice at the flaming crucible stake.

Allow it to be stated for all posterity as such here upon this page,
that the greatest crucible exists by our determination to take direct specific action,

separating those among whom are possessed
by the hallowed spirit of immortal freedom,
from those among the inactive and non-possessed
whom exist among the weakest in intellectual
capacity and superlative genes,
who therefore in their unwillingness to stand by
faithfully during the dawning age of immense sacrifice,
consequently forfeit their position to stand during the time
of our forthcoming victory jubilee celebration..
in outstanding anticipation of receiving the eternal reward thereof.
Those who choose not to labor in honorable service
to the coming new Kingdom Of God,
then choose to labor in their own eternal enforced servitude.

There indeed exists no middle ground
in the coming Kingdom Of The Sacred Divine!
Those whom do not labor for the resurrection,
then choose their own immutable subjugation.
Should one then still choose to forfeit
his sacrificial offering of labor and talent,
then he shall choose to offer his very life,
his service rendered in the form of products
derived from his mortal body,
then sold in departments existing deep
within the incarcerating system
or on the universal market at large.

Behold,
in the dawning Kingdom Of The Original Superlative,
there exists no middle ground,
no room for stagnating complacency,
no decision for neutrality bearing the insidious expectation of reaping

the reward from those who chose to make the grand
hallowed sacrifice.

For there does exist only the immortal compulsion for
productive action,
the swelling desire for superlative accomplishment that
shall endlessly neutralize all desire for idle complacency and the
slothful desire for gratuitous accommodation,
rendering that individual as an impediment
to all future superlative advancement.
In the name of advancing the neo Kingdom
Of Technological Elysium,
mankind shall stand steadfast to expunge
that negative repressive element
from within his midst!

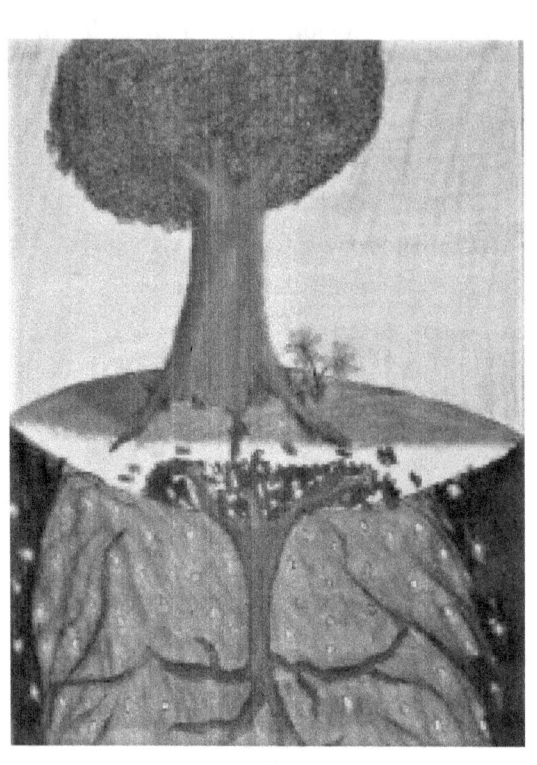

THE HERMIT

(the redeeming justification)

Behold,
The time for our own self acknowledgment has presently arrived.
All mortal earth must realize, grasp, and acknowledge our dominating presence.
We stand as the precious remnants of the immortal original,
the renowned superlative precursor unto all men who thus developed in our wake.

Our place of immaculate origin was on the distant planet,
Summus Nebiru.
While on that planet we lived within an outstanding technological paradise,
then something horrible happened.
Our population exploded, since life was so good there.
Our extraordinary wealth led to an over exploitation of the planet's resources.
Within a few millennium our people were nearing starvation and horrendous poverty,
the situation bearing the only valid solution
as being to reduce the population
beneath the rate of the planets resource production.
While violence was one possibility,
we were far above stooping down into that base level of thought.

In addition to the above,
our people as they were within themselves,
were not a threat unto our own future advancement,
nor did they exist as dead weight impediments
who only consumed without contribution,
expecting gratuitous accommodation at our own systemic expense,

like blood sucking parasites who feed from the national body,
only weakening it down for the external predators to attack;
thus the need for permanent extermination did not exist.

We were in possession of the supreme technology
to devise an alternative solution,
so in lieu of that dominating fact,
our wise-men could deduce that the proper solution was to simply relocate.
Our astrologers and wise-men gazed
far and wide throughout the celestial universe
in search of a planet that most resembled our old homeland.
Soon we were to discover the one that was almost a perfect match,
and of course,
that planet was the emerald earth.

From afar,
in every way did the planet earth resemble our Summis Nebiru,
the firmament between the seas and the land,
the very seas themselves!
The teaming life beneath the waves !
The plant and animal life on the land!

In most cases,
we were familiar with it all,
the life itself bearing some but few differences!
Upon our study of the history,
we could easily deduce the reason as to why this was so.

Deep into the distant celestial past,
our planet had once smashed into earth,
ripping out nearly two thirds of the entire planet.

These massive empty spaces were soon filled by the blood of the earth,
forming all of the oceans.

With that colossal act of violence,
some of the soil from Summus Nibiru was heaped upon the remaining
land.
That historical fact explains why the plant life and the animal life
of the northern regions on earth most resembles
that which we have left behind.

In addition to the above,
a massive chunk of soil from the carving of the earth
was cast high into the heavens surrounding it.
It was soon caught up in the gravitational influence of the earth,
causing it to orbit.
The solar wind isotopes that it passed through in it's orbit caused it
to form a sphere,
upon which it then behaved as a sub planet,
later known as *Luna*.

Future generations of mortals would become amazed at the fact of water
being added into their primitive samples of the soil from *Luna*,
and the vegetable herbs of earth flourishing in it without any nutritional
additives.
Now the reason for this old fact has been made public for all to analyze!

Following
our investigation from above and
the investigation bearing the historical facts,
we then,
according to the laws of deductive reasoning and logic,
were obligated to support these factual revelations with an actual manned
exploratory mission,

for the purpose of gathering scientific data for our further deductive analysis
in determining as to whether or not the earth was appropriate for
our future colonization.

In that deductive analysis,
all facts must be held into accountability and gathered from
a very broad area upon the face of the earth.
According to the deductive analysis that was made,
there were some twelve planets investigated and earth was the most
logical choice.

Specifically on the face of the earth,
the northern extremities were most suited for our habitation;
that fact being stated,
however,
our superlative nature is to be extremely adaptable,
effectively allowing us to survive and thrive in virtually *any* environment,
no matter how inhospitable.

Our beginnings would take place where life
was most simple for us to engage.
This conclusion was made in lieu
of the deductive logic that preceded it.
Bear in mind here as well,
that the deduction was based upon hard verifiable facts.

Another fact determined from our astrological investigation
was that our home planet came closest in orbit to earth on January 5th,
every three millennium.
With that fact bore the suggestion
that the most logical time for colonization
would be on January 5th.

Some four tri-millennium ago we waited
until the appropriate time.
Just prior to that exact date,
within the preceding month,
we sent another manned mission to investigate the conditions,
first within the hemisphere at large,
then within our specific targeted area.
This targeted area was a large solid peninsula
jutting from the banks of the mainland
into an expansive sea known as *Morimaru* by our endowed
astrologers and scientific investigative researchers.

At that appointed time the peninsula
did not possess any surrounding islands.
The logic preceding our choice was that first,
the peninsula teamed with life within
and in the seas without.

Next the choice was preceded by the fact
that the great sea offered protection,
when it was certain to be needed in the distant future,
according to our predetermining logic in presumption.

The isolated context of the peninsula
would consequently allow our culture to develop
into a superlative maximum,
in complete adaptation to the surrounding natural environment.

The location of the peninsula being
somewhat central within the total landmass,
and yet possessing such great diversity
and abundance of resources,
allowed for an outstanding cultural development first within,

then for a future radiating advancement without,
therefore guaranteeing that we would thrive and prosper
for all future time into infinity!

Following our manned investigative research into the peninsula,
our analytical investigators concluded
that some surrounding islands would be nice,
not only for a recreational tourist break from the established routine,
but for a future strategic buffer zone
against any type of future threat from abroad.

Islands would also encourage the growth of wildlife,
both within the sea among them and on the land.
This new development would provide
both for basic subsistence and future trade.

As a result of this deductive determination,
our astrologers determined to simply divert an asteroid
into the peninsula.
This asteroid was one well chosen that consisted mainly of ice
and highly nutrient rich space dust,
minus of any radioactive material,
but yet containing some metals that would serve as later trade items
for our people to build their wealth upon,
for later high tech developments that we could deduce
would be certain to arrive in some distant future time frame,
but would not presently contaminate the environment.

These metals,
when consumed by the surrounding wildlife,
would also mutate their genes in a manner
that our researchers had deduced
would enhance the game stock by leading to the

future development of entirely new game species
that would cause the surrounding environment
to enhance and propagate itself,
rather than destroy.

This fact is the reason that the game and livestock there,
as well as the production rate of our herbs and vegetables,
even to this very day,
is so much meatier and richer in taste;
as well as being much more productive
than that from any other areas on earth,
until those areas fell under our future influence.

By use of a simple pressure based abrupt release
on the side of the asteroid
facing our desired point of direction,
which caused the solar wind to expand only on that side,
a powerful vacuum was then created only on that side.

The asteroid then moved over to fill this vacuum,
which created a void on the other side of the asteroid,
that when the solar wind contracted to fill,
behaved more as a catapult that hurled the asteroid
directly into the peninsula with great speed.

Hence,
the asteroid slammed into the peninsula
and shattered it along the edges into a
number of small surrounding islands.

The mathematical logic that facilitated
this great feat was very simple;
a three mile diameter asteroid hurled

at twelve thousand light years per second,
would certainly facilitate an explosion
that would accomplish this most outstanding feat
in superlative objective.

This massive feat was accomplished
only a single tri-millennium
from the time that we had predetermined
to colonize the landscape.

Thus
on January 5th,
twelve thousand years ago,
we made our first landing in mass.
By that time the earth had effectively healed itself.
The effect of our efforts was exceptionally magnificent to behold!
Our grand efforts and colossal manifestations even astounded ourselves..!

Even unto this very day,
only the remaining ruins astound
what are passed off as being "gifted" researchers.
In fact,
if these researchers were truly blessed
by the anointed wisdom of the superlative ancients,
then they would bear no fear
and simply speak exactly of the past
suggested by our magnificent ruins,
rather than only stand idly by
and allow the facts to be simply ignored
in favor of the base lie,
that man and the very earth beneath his feet,
ascended from a grossly base inferior into a superlative!

How is it that mortal academia
could be so ignorant as to accept such a claim
that so blatantly violates basic logic and reasoning?
What is their self serving intention
in making this ludicrous claim?
Whom is it that has placed these imbeciles upon their payroll,
only to pass them off as wise men
bearing anointed scientific knowledge?
Can the gold in their salary be
traced back to the reigning authority?

If so,
then how is it that they themselves
can be served in this affront
to basic reason and logic?
An ascendancy cannot exist in lieu of a corruption!
Corruption always leads into an eroding descendant,
no matter if the target is animate or inanimate!

……..Behold
our mighty metropolis ruins
beneath the very center of the deepest seas
that stand in superlative violation to their outrageous claims of
man-kind and the very earth itself ascending from an inferior!
We are greatly amused
that even their most gifted wise men
cannot effectively explain this reality,
so they respond by simply ignoring an ever looming phenomenon,
while they continue to hammer their pathetic lies into
into the minds of their innocent children!

…….. Behold
the ancient sagas that speak of our predecessors

being mighty men of accomplished renown,
many proudly standing more than three meters tall,
their lives being ruled by unadulterated logic and reason,
while they spend their days basking in scientific discovery
and all of the creative arts,
as well as the massive wealth that was derived
from trading enterprising endeavors.

. . . .Behold
our mighty warrior culture that once extended
from the heartland of Europa,
moving eastward across the Mediterranean lands,
conquering all of the Asian transcendence,
on into great Asia itself,
all resistance melting before us as we advanced unopposed across
norther India and even deep into the farthermost
reaches of northern Zhongguo!
Here, both we ourselves, and our
superlative warrior culture, dominated
for more than three millennium!

. . . . . . .Behold
the so called wise men of today
discover our mummies by the thousands in that
vast area where our kindred once reigned supreme!
In their prevailing ignorance
they know not what to make of this outstanding phenomenon.
No matter what they shout and say,
there lay our once gloriously crafted bodies,
enshrouded in locks of still glittering
crimson and gold!
The great warrior's cape still is gracing their backs as they lay,
to the right of their tombs lays their swords in the cherished X sign,

across the X lay their arrows and javelin tips.
In the very midst of this reigning star
is carefully placed their intricately embossed shields,
all lain to bear the precious star
and cross sign of the genetic superlative. . ..,
the sign of the star betrays their place of origin,
the swords and the javelin tips betraying their supremacy in battle,
all of this elegant decoration bearing
the timeless mark of supremacy in the creative arts!
Thus for three thousand years
we constructed and developed intellectually
to such a great extent that our efforts astounded all of the nether men
who surrounded us.
Their legends still praise our sanctified greatness,
even to this very day!

Behold unto all men,
in those days of long lost yore,
all that we knew was eternal peace,
outwardly radiating glory in our superlative artistic and intellectual creativity,
intertwined with our illustrious prosperity beyond all mortal imagination!

But
the dark lord of the negative superlative
became extremely jealous of the fact that a creation
of the positive superlative could become so advanced and
accomplished to such an illustrious degree.

So
he caused the very elements within the earth
and the light of the sun without
to curse the life flow of the positive superlative's master creation.

The elements of their blood reacted to form mutations,
which were then passed down unto the following generation,
where it manifested itself as horrible disease
and destructive negative tendencies;
such as:
slothfulness,
unfaithfulness,
lust of men for other men,
disregard for logic and reason in favor of assumption,
covetousness,
tendency for theft,
a lying tongue,
a hatred and disregard for what is holy,
lacking the ability to love,
lack of creativity and imagination,
tendencies for additive behavior,
the *inability to moderate. . ..*

To this very day,
when we observe families,
we can readily view these negative tendencies
when they are passed down by inheritance,
and many more
that betray the recent corruption of inherited genes
by the fact that the carrier does not have to labor at the negative tendency.

All positive tendencies,
which were in the original possession of the genetic superlative,
must be labored upon constantly
in order to maintain their development potential
and their superlative qualities.
This sole fact in observation is verification
of their distance from that original superlative.

On the outset
of this base corruption,
those infected genes only existed
within isolated family pockets
and very few in number.

The negative lord of the dark knew well their
weakness for debauchery,
thus in some,
the mutated gene carried with it the disregard for reason
and logic,
thereby certain individuals lost the capacity
to withhold from the motivation of the most basic
of biological urges,
and the result was to crossbreed within their own
immediate families,
which then resulted in the creation of more mutated genes,
as well as greatly multiplying those that were already in existence!
This occurrence is how the already tainted bloodlines
became even more tainted at an ever increased rate.

In numerous cases,
some corrupted individuals were only carriers,
while numerous others bore
resulting negativity in it's totality.
These carriers grew to be the great men of ancient renown
that the oldest sagas tell such tales of glory in their travels,
wisdom and accomplishments.
Unfortunately
those dormant carriers who became
the outstanding adventurers of ancient renown,
also took a liking towards the daughters of the lucid superlative,
and they crossbred,

producing spawn that possessed only original positive traits,
with some few only possessing the obvious negative traits and
bearing those strange birth defects
and apparent diseases born from mutated corrupting genes.

All of whom came into contact with
the infected inherently
became tainted themselves,
existing only as carriers
if not bearing the full blown obvious diseases,
personality negatives, and gross
behaviors born from the genetic corruption.

As other lucid families witnessed their daughters
and their blood lines becoming
contaminated when coming in contact with those
tainted family and individual bloods,
the scholarly minded intellectual elders
among the lucid patriarchs wisely forbade integration,
especially among their impressionable youth.

In many territories citizens were forbidden
to interrelate with individuals
from certain specific areas and later on,
from certain specific families,
especially when suddenly upon exposure and crossbreeding,
the remaining lucid elders bore witness to an increase in crime,
particularly vicious crime
that defied all logic and explanation,
existing in combination with a general loss
in the conception of resourcefulness.

Those whom possessed tainted bloods were contented
to impose themselves on those among the lucid,
their infected masses continuing to flood
into areas that were strictly forbidden for them to enter.
This action of disregard on part of those individuals
bearing the tainted blood inheritance
is the sole motivation that eventually led
to those horrible savage conflicts
and wars that the infinite sagas speak so much of;
all of this dawning evil in lands where only scientific knowledge
and creative intellectual development were previously known;
war and conflict existing with contrary criminal personality
were socially deteriorating elements that
were previously unknown,
until the times of the great contaminating blood infection.

In the
celestial heights of high heaven above,
that omniscient master of the positive superlative,
the great and mighty
Ahuramazda,
gazed down upon the base debauchery of his
outstanding superlative creation,
and the consequential destruction thereof.

Although he was eternally wise to the fact that the lord of the negative
had engineered the base destruction of his magnificent
creation,
what disappointed him most of all was the fact that he had bestowed upon
that creation,
the gift of superlative reason and the ability to make deductions based on
factual observation,
thereby *always* arriving at the exact valid conclusion.

In this manner,
the proper response would be to perceive the preemptive consequence
of giving in to a base motivation of biology
or the exiting need for new adventure,
and simply withhold from following through on the motivation.

The weakness of his precious superlative creation
in withholding from the motivation to go through the motion of procreation,
except when within the realm of the ordained regulations,
was what truly disappointed him most of all.
The supreme reason of this outstanding disappointment,
was that out of all of the possible base actions,
the act of debauchery led to the future destruction of the entire society
and even the individual people themselves,
with the destruction being very subtle as the wealth of the targeted society
and the social industriousness simply melts away gradually over time.

The end result is always extreme poverty and grinding deprivation,
hence guaranteeing social destruction for centuries,
even millennium beyond.

The only
hope for those whom exist within this catastrophic dark veil would
be the redemption by a superlative celestial intervention,
bearing the intention of resurrecting the original superlative blood.

It was for this sole reason
that the ancient prophets told of in the oldest sagas,
spoke of the emergence on earth concerning the supreme magnificent messiah,
hailing from that distant solar realm,

Nifleheim,
that most immaculate star existing closest to the planet Summus Nibiru.

Some nine feet tall he shall stand they say,
appearing first as a mortal child,
but arising through his own genius intellectual strategic deductions
and incessant efforts,
into a commanding supremacy among all mortal men.

Not only shall he direct the actions of mortals,
but he shall direct even their very thoughts,
standing before them to radiate his consuming spirit through the palm
of his raised right hand.

At his very command,
which is both heard but even more so,
felt
within the hearts of all men in possession of the supreme,
until it prompts an astounding motivation to rise up in complete majestic
order,
when the precious symbol of their forthcoming genetic resurrection
rises to the surface beneath their feet
and in illustrious standard before their very eyes,
beckoning their very inner spirits,
those possessed spirits of their ancient superlative ancestors,
to provoke dedicated action
in combination with the supreme in altruistic conflagration
and consecrated sacrifice,
to motivate for the ultimate world conquest. . ..

Forth from their massive mountain top Bastille
they all shall stand in glorious formation of the radiating Thunder Sun,
to march forth upon mankind,

giving ceaseless battle to the destructive venara-men and the nether-mortals
existing within the midst of superlative man-kind,
bearing only the insidious intention to destroy both humanity within,
and the superlative emerald earth without;
their forthright intention being to march forward in total absence of hesitating complacency,
and purge the entire earth of the base putrefying parasitic nether-man presence
and culture.

According to the ancient prophets
we would know this messiah by his
illustrious motivating worldwide actions,
but also by the fact that his only opposition
would be a mortal completely
possessed by the spirit of the dark superlative,
who would rise above all men
and stand to oppose him,
only to be defeated in an all consuming world conflagration,
later being captured,
then condemned to crucifixion
on the bare granite heights of Megiddo,
on the alter point of universal celestial knowledge
standing at the center of emerald earth.
Every eye on mortal earth shall bear witness to the execution,
young and old,
male and female.

Then shall the great deliverer stand
forward on this high majestic mount,
before the wreathing,
crucified body,
raising both his hands high,

speaking unto all men concerning the ordained destiny of men
and all of emerald earth without.

As the speech is rendered,
lightening shall strike forth from the skies
upon the crucified body
of the dark demigod,
rendering it into flames before all of mortal earth.
It shall be this sole celestial manifested occurrence that shall
confirm the identity of the divine one,
our majestic positive superlative deliverer!

And
his name shall be called;
The Immaculate,
The Timeless One,
The Perfect One who knows no imperfection,
nor bears any by blood or endeavor!
There shall come a day soon
when all the earth shall stand and
hail the great magnificent redeemer,
beholding the immaculate son of almighty
Ahuramazda. . ..
and his name shall be called
Zorothrausi,
the supreme celestial deliverer,
son of the luminescent positive genetic superlative!

Among the pages
within those consecrated scriptures of the timeless sagas,
it is said that we would all know of his nearing triumphant emergence,
when all of man-kind endorsed the tainting of those bloods

existing closest to the superlative,
with those of the simea-men who exist farthermost from the original superlative.

This base endorsement will be worldwide,
entwined within the ruling *all inclusive* doctrinaire
sponsored by the governments of earth,
designed to spread the profits of superlative endeavor to supplant the corroding
putrefaction of purgeman wastefulness
and general lacking of industriousness,
only to be forcefully imposed upon those laboring masses of subjugated men,
then referred to only as citizens of planet earth.

Even the earth itself will reject this tainted embrace,
for in those days it will reel in it's orbit as one who walks
and is highly inebriated.
The seas will reel to and fro in raging waves
that will slay thousands upon thousands.

In many places fire and brimstone will fall
from the heights of high heaven above to slay
men in numbers that even they themselves cannot begin to fathom.
The prevailing weather of earth will continually heat
in an effort of earth to purge
itself of man-kind's corroding curse by timeless crucible of fire. . .

The final blasphemous insult
will be when the ruling governments of men strike the name
of the great and powerful from all of their architect
and literature,
teaching their corrupting lies to their most impressionable youth;
only to replace his gracious name even in their very midst,

with the name of a figure in dominating statue
that stands to represent their insidious corroding all inclusive government
and their future intent in imposing worship of this vile entity
on the masses of mortal earth.

Behold all of mortal earth,
the name of this repulsive entity in statue shall be called;
Qui Dat Munera

By then the massive
diverging crucible will have already been established,
that crucible of technological innovation which separates those in minority
who are brilliantly successful and accomplished,
in spite of the massive displacement of workers,
from those who are endless failures
doomed to only sink beneath the rising waves of new technology
and innovation.

The great crucible of technology
will serve to effectively separate those born of divine superlative genes
from the genetic mutant inferiors.

Their shining success will demonstrate all of the fine
attributes of the positive genetic superlative;
such as a well developed imagination,
high level of reason and logic capacity,
anointed in natural entrepreneur development skills and desire,
a very strong desire to succeed at all costs,
the tendency for scientific investigation and discovery.

The insidious new rule of government
will become established to service the

inferior majority,
whom only exist as the failures of humanity and nature,
at the purloined expense of the positive genetic superlative
who thrive as those of pure destiny and innovation
on the face of the earth,
entrusted with the radiant advancement of the emerald sphere
and all of the divine creations therein. . .,

who stand to radiate forth
as the highly skilled and successful self made
healers,
scientists,
discoverers of new medicine,
discovers of new technology,
the great creative painters,
creative magicians,
extraordinarily successful business owners,
the great classical musicians,
the great mathematicians who make new ingenious discoveries. . .
and innumerable others of the same illustrious breed.

The immortal
Zorothrausi
will serve as vindicating messiah unto this cherished element,
leading them forward into an immaculate superlative greatness unlike no other
seen before them nor will follow after them.
In great triumph he will lead them forward
to crucify that adorned demigod of the fruitless nether-mortals,
Magna Latro!

Following this great flaming crucifixion,
destined to be witnessed by all the earth,

then and only then will come the mighty realm transforming speech,
announcing unto all the earth that the time of divine deliverance has arrived,
and then following by giving them all their proper instructions for action,
all to march forward with a mighty triumphant air to relinquish the nether-mortals
and the neather-men from the limbs of
those now in minority most deserving of the supreme rewards
born from superlative inclination, skill, brilliantly creative minds
and dedicated labor,
for all time thereafter.
What shall follow the colossal deliverance
will be a time of jubilation and unrestrained prosperity like none
that the emerald earth has even imagined during it's most detailed induced vision. . .

Behold. . .,
No more extortionist fees,
no more repressive regulation,
no more lies about our precious heritage that must always
follow to give support to the extortionist regime.
Vain pseudoscience will then be replaced by claims
supported with hard verifiable facts,
since the false regime of the sub-humans has
now been effectively destroyed and
the need to justify it in the minds of the masses
dramatically eliminated.
Eternal peace will once again return to emerald earth,
since vain jealousy spawned by unrestrained sub-human covetousness
has now been indefinitely erased from the face of all mankind,
destined to be replaced by joyful innovation
and illustrious creativity radiating an intense jubilation
in the anointed ability to intellectually research,
design and create!

*No more disease that was once caused by immoderate behavior,
only to be spread throughout humanity by nether-mortal inconsideration,
and that of their supporting regime,
who forced all others to accept their integration in an attempt to neutralize
the prevailing sub-human face on the disease itself.*

Most importantly,
our precious men and women will no longer be forced to feel compulsion
by the enemy ruling regime of the nether-mortal,
to procreate with him in their vain war
against logic and sound analytical reasoning.
The innate tendency to observe and deduce,
then support their conclusion of deduction with
a clear valid plan of action, is the greatest threat to their true intention,
which is to enslave the entire mass of humanity;
Hence,
The very best slave made
is the slave who is enchained,
yet is convinced from the bottom of his very soul
that he is free;
such is only possible
when he posses no eyes with which to see!

Behold
all subordinate humanity of emerald earth,
we whom exit within the realm of the genetic superlative
do posses eyes and we most certainly do see,
and what we don't readily see standing immediately before us
we can conclusively deduce. . .!
So the vain swine shall never deceive us..!
We stand before thee and hereby declare holy war
on ye and all of ye vile efforts to purloin our lavish lifestyles and wealth,
only to redistribute it back out unto thy sub-human dregs!

Hark ye now,
oh ye vile ones of mortal earth!
Oh ye scourge of the vegetative green,
tremble in thy boots until thy knees knocketh together
and thy very bones shatter into pieces!

On those vast courtyard parade grounds
in the colossal Bastille of high Montem Dei
at the very center of the reeling earth,
we now stand in our proud radiating sun formation,
marching forward to the reigning commands of our
prophesied anointed leader,
to the glorious ancient sign of the radiant Thunder Sun,
that speaks precious words into our awakened ears
and even into our very yearning souls,
valiantly announcing our forthcoming complete conquest
and domination of all emerald earth.
Hail to the march of the divine nine mil!

Ride through all the earth bearing the destructive speed of a raging tempest!
Strike fear into astounded hearts and minds like the force of a consuming conflagration!
Render the sub-human species and their repugnant culture
into the dust of the earth for all eternity,
permanently erase their repulsive memory
from the pages of our blessed history in beseech.
Allow the pages of our blessed redemptive testimony
commence even on this very moment!
Serving in radiant glory to eternally replace that most abominable stain
with the glittering culture and illustrious creativity
of a new engendering technological era..,
hail to the dawning era of the Divine Magnificent!

WHEEL OF FORTUNE

The time
of thy birth is mine,
the moment of thy first cry I approved;
the incident of thy first step was my sign.
Unto thee goeth my silent blessing. . . . .,
behoove!

The moment
of the great event is only thine
by my sacred address to the proper elemental testing,
of those negative circumstances and threatening spiritual elements soon
removed,
thus the moment of the occurrence shall be initiated
into blessed serenity.

On the very moment of thy first hart slain,
salute!,
my discerning eye and the twinkling stars above,
we both knew.

The very first
luscious lips to fall into thy enraptured embrace
amid the heart throbbing whims of thy timid puppy love,
only occurred when we both approved.

High
in the twinkling midnight sky
the hunter raced into the deep blue,
far beyond the great divide,
to seize the enchanted lariat from the Wizard Woo,

to slice the tarnished section of the pie
still clutched in the right hand of the dancing moon.

Thus
whilst consumed within those actions,
when the die at those backroom tables flew,
they only did so by our consolidated sanction.

So thus
when thy mighty knights and bold heroes rode forth
into the dismal somber mists beyond,
they were only successful because we both were moved,
guiding their thoughts and the advantageous movements of their horse.

Of the future we are behooved,
let the past lay not in thy bitter regret for the worst,
for it is toward a most glorious future that the superlative shall be wooed.

For I tell thee all
that the stars are right to set the venerated mood,
and thy chariots shall now sound of brace and harness strap,
and the ride of the brilliant nine mil shall never forestall,
even amid the enemy's mightiest bomb blasts,
and the strength that our divine march shall surly sap!

For thy vanquishing
destiny is written even in the stars above,
when Jupiter shall ore Venus move,
when Orion shall race afar underneath,
then around them all shall Taurus groove,
never concerned with the consequences in the least!

Look!
There appeareth
the intrepid unicorn
unto mighty Taurus beseech,
in future wisdom and technology to seek;
Then cometh Cancer and Capricorn bearing thy sacred book,
casting form thy charms and spells to make the arrogant among thee meek.

From the skies above assails Gemini,
to grant wisdom unto the fool and might unto thy weak;
seeking to transform all fantastic idealism and irrationality,
into positive calculating strategy.

Moving forth
to bestow blessed imagination upon thy dismal bleak,
conquering all strategic investments born by the enemy's regency.
Then shall come mighty Ares
and her adoring Danaan children,
to dazzle the opposition in ways to make the tide vary,
from even the bloodiest dismal into the most jubilant cheerful,
when
the new orange sun shall upward round the tree-lined distance without!

So now at thy anointed feet
shall purl the ancient amber creek,
those immaculate pixie about shall gather and speak
unto thy children whom in the distant future seek
the quiet secret of thy valor and tales of the world consuming war so bleak,
and the total conquest of thy enemy now so complete.

For the nature of the enemy's face they wish to see,
those evil ones who sought to repress all future liberty
and our lavish serenity.

Security they then sought in perpetual knowledge
that the dreadful enemy was rendered into blood drenched carnage,
mere dust beneath their tender playful feet.
For then all will dwell in thy Elysium so sweet,
thy ancient masters now rendered into eternal shame and defeat.
Where only thy illustrious enterprise shall reign supreme,
thy astounding architecture and creative inventions shall offer their iridescent gleam!

The entire gem of emerald earth shall then be thy solid embrace,
thy sorrows forever gone without a trace.
Twas us,
the constellation stars and the tarot speak,
into our clouded mist centered in thy crystal orbs ye seek,
ye gaze forth into thy palms and for our secret knowledge ye pine,
for thy courage gained and the will to pursue shall be thine,
thy purposeful minds shall thus on a single point be fixed,
compelling even thy weary limbs through those marshy travails and thorny sticks.

To a vexing heart, weary and weak,
The elation of victory, the sight of enemy defeat,
the ring of our sword, the sight of their flowing blood—so sweet,
We shall gaze forth upon those shattered fields of struggle,
our faces covered with tears of shear joy as we stand and weep!

Listen
to the sound of the whispering breeze,
behold the flock of birds floating with such ease,

feel the message in the flocks that heralds an unseen presence?
Gaze upon thy pond reflection covered in spring time essence,
endeavor to enter inside thy reflections midst,
the sacred trance shall envelope thy mind as thy silent ardor enlists
those deepest secrets from our spirits and pixie spritz.
The voices of both the raven the raging crow
of thy future fortune they doeth know.

Behold the ardor and flow of the entire earth without,
thy mathematicians posses thy coveted knowledge and the clout,
to cipher thy fortune and relay the secret wisdom that the gods so graciously confer.
Give light unto thy sacred oaken yule tide fires...
gaze forth into the dark smoke ascending,
thus the trance shall consume to invigorate thy deepest desire.,
giving insight to exhalt thy fortunate ending.

Then at long last
all of the emerald earth behold
the majestic return of the superlative grand.

Even within the earth itself,
the blessed word was foretold.
Into an ever increasing heat all the earth was cast,
the numbers of men swelled until all wealth ran cold.
The strength of the earth grew wane because the extraction was vast!

The parasite man,
like those on thy mongrel grew,
until the body groweth weak and
of dreadful pestilence it soon knew
that some seventy percent of those on the cur

merciful fate slew;
Thus preserved the body and the precious resources within.

Hence
It is only justified that all of those remaining that stand
should exist among the ranks of the superlative grand!
The thundering voice of the entire earth is loudly proclaiming
that the long awaited anointed time is at hand.
The fierce seas and the conflicting currents within,
the raging skies and the howling winds
that wreak such horrible destruction upon men.
The trembling of the earth and the spewing volcanoes without,
the violent changing of the weather
and thy precious crops that hang their heads and pout.

Mortal men
behold in all of these fateful signs,
there is wisdom to learn,
the time is near at hand for their superlative return!

THE HANGED MAN

Behold
all mortal men,
the anointed moment of thy blessed
redemption hath now arrived,
as was prophesied by our superlative fore-bearers
in the most ancient of sages.

Were we not
first created and granted rightful position
among the mortal creation supreme?
The time of our astounding new birth
hath arrived!

Consider this,
must we eternally submit unto
the negative declivity that hath been so
callously thrust upon us,
even to the point that it destroys all of humanity
and emerald earth itself?

In continuing decay
and dreadful decadence,
must we continue to eternally wallow in the putrid filth
and mire of those mutated negative ?

Allow thy blazing celestial bronze trumpets
to blast throughout all of mortal emerald earth!
The time for our astounding metamorphosis
hath now arrived!

In the name of supreme altruism we,
the mortals of emerald earth,
shall sacrifice our bodies in our total inclusiveness
on the alter of supreme creativity and
illustrious positive accomplishments!

Hence,
we shall then shed our mutated bodies and be made whole again!
Then shall we enter thus into the birthing millennium,
with genuine crafted bodies divine that glow in radiating strength,
permanently endowed with our anointed creativity,
our investigative wisdom based on
the most unadulterated of conclusive logic.

Existing proudly within our most perfect Elysium serenity. . ..
Indefinitely free from the grasp of inherited disease and birth defects,
and the vice grip of illness and it's gross tendency.
Living at large
with the very best that can ever possibly be
when ye shall strive effectively to eternally sever thy
mutated bonds with those repressive spirits bearing
the most confining chains of. . .;

G*reed,*
which eternally corrodes and destroys the cherished positive
spirit of giving and brotherly love;

Lust,
the bane of all true love,
the truest of life pleasure in it's superlative dress;

Slothfulness,
the purloin of all personal wealth and
the base of societal decay predicting eventual ruin;

Deceit,
the true bane of future advancement,
both
to thy person and thy kingdom at large;

Wrath,
for it gives way unto foolish haste,
thy energy taken and thy resources shall lay waste;

Pride,
which shall surly woo thy forthcoming vulnerability;

Envy,
stands as the hallmark of the insolent simian-man whom
detest the illustrious accomplishments of the superlative grand;

Gluttony,
betrays the mutated gene for immoderation,
the bane of tactful strategy to overcome looming adversity.

With
the dividing crucible now
seated in it's solid place,
heralding the astounding separation
between superlative efficiency and inferior waste,
those whom shall sacrifice all in the name
of humanity's sweet superlative exaltation.
By crucible of sword and calcimine flame
the blessed action shall not make further haste remorseful blame ;

for the end result exalted shall harbinger the heavenly spirits joyous glee
. . .
Forsooth. . .,
from the eroding burden of consuming squandering men shall the earth then
be eternally free!

The established exalted millennium
for all infinity shall thus be thy reconsecration,
the paradise created shall extend great joyful popularity
to propagate thy superlative prosperity!

Brotherly love and
adoration for procreating family shall once again
reign supreme,
their corrupting enemies
eternally cast forth into the flaming extreme. . ..

Thence
every weeping eye shall in it's tearful rain indefinitely cease,
all earthly peace then restored and thy mortal ease,
thy slinking feline shall lay with the tarnishing mouse,
the raging flame shall then spare thy mortal house;
the cat shall appeal to the hare in heaving remorse,
begging forgiveness from his former persecuting coerce.
Thence shall the thief cease in his vile begets,
for the mutated gene thus removed will validate his request.

The base desire for blood
and all unsanctioned lusts,
the permanent removal of the mutated gene will entrust
that the body and soul will flee from even the most base of pernicious desire,
as both the hart and the hare do the deep forest flood.

Men will thence be given only unto women,
the corrupted gene rendered thence unto the crucible furnace unforgiving;
Only the most lucid love for blessed devotion and family reign supreme,
thy soul intrinsic purpose to repopulate emerald earth with our excellent being!

Ore the all of emerald earth
shall then the little bear reign in it's precious anointed supreme!
Our cherished isolated Elysium abode resurrected from deep within the vile enthrall,
bearing our divinely bestowed opulence and luxuriant glittering stream.

Thence
in that day of the lucid resurrected divinity
shall return the hallowed age of ancient Ares,
when those blessed angelic beings of that wisest order
shall dwell in perfect serenity.

Behold. . . . .
the positions of those heavenly stars. . . . .,
the incessant increasing force of the distant howling winds. . . . .,
the strength and frequency of typhoon tempest at sea. . ..,
the mighty shaking of the earth beneath thy timid feet. . . . .,
the gradual warming of the earths' interior. . . . .,
the seas slowly swallowing distant majestic shores
that were exposed during the time of their retreat
from the cherished firmament. . .. . .;
The sweltering population on earth and the vanishing of
their nourishing, sustaining resources. . .. . . .
The horrors of those seething rages that rise in jealous covetousness,
fueling wars more terrible than those of any prior age. . . . .

the increasing beseech of men for divine assistance
toward those most majestic wardens
of the celestial heights. . . . .

. . . . ..Raise thy despairing faces
toward the heavens in mighty triumphant cheer. . .!
. . .For the anointed time
of their marvelous manifestation draweth near..!

Let the enrapturing word
freedom
ring once again throughout thy enchanting land. . .;

Hail
to the divine march of the Superlative Grand!

DEATH

From the very onset
I was there,
both to transcend the souls
of those baneful tarnished and the fair!

Forth
from the confines of mortal tribulations
and despair,
into those most enchanting realms
of brilliant gold and imagination of the rare
in illustrious opulence and pleasures of glittering life,
perpetually free of opposing travail and incessant strife.

When the blessed infant
Zorothrausi
lay slumbering in thy stony cave cleft
in the midst of that raging den of lions,
shielded from all harm by the mighty hand of the all powerful,
Ahuramazda,
I was there!
Condemning only the oppressing enemies
into the eternal realm of ethereal ghosts,
denying them all access to their gracious persecuted hosts.

Though engrossed by outstanding
strength and the most lucid health,
they only melted in their sadistic quest
by silent forces of pestilence in perfect stealth.

As the anointed infant grew
he was to attend the league of the immortal twelve

forward into the land of those cursed Koloss giants,
much plunder did they secure
and some thirty of the tarnished raging villains they slew.

Early on as a natural born leader of men he did shine,
for his age at the time of this great feat was only around nine.
With the hand of the Almighty offering him his protection,
I could only make do with those whom stood outside of his divine affection.
In the arts of wisdom and knowledge he did command
all of those surrounding with his in-depth perception to understand.
Soon the very head position of their academies he did occupy,
and any who silently thought to oppose him never offered a try.

I was there
when the all encompassing dividing crucible
was established in it's place,
and the skills of the laboring people
were rendered worthless throughout all time and space;
when the wrenching squalor
and privation made it's disparaging squeeze,
I was there.

When the righteous and the beautiful turned to sleaze,
I was there.

When the
colossal masses chose thy entrancing herbs
in exchange of thy intellectual superb,
I was there.

When the
rejected soon felt so despised,

tumbling so deeply over into thy expansive
distant gloomy horizon,
soon to embrace the bony hand of suicide,
I was there.

When thy
prophesied anointed leader arose,
giving potent stir unto thy masses once reposed,
now motivated into thy superlative future of heaven's fare,
hence
my blessing was to see it all.

When thy
sanctified climax shall then appear at long last,
thy mutated body will thy then have cast
into that timeless gloom and flame,
offered in holy sacrifice for thy glorious name!
Through it all
my name will still be fare,
up until that moment when thy supreme paradise shall spare
from thy presence and my diadem from thy mortal care.

Thus. . ..
now thy great sacrifice will hath been made,
thy ancient body rendered into the eternal grave,
now bestowed thy new body radiating in heaven's gleam.
Thy new ascendancy into thy most elegant supreme
stand. . ..

Hail
to the march of the Superlative Grand!

TEMPERANCE AND THE RISING SUN

When that day of splendid magnificence shall then appear,
all restraints of repressive regulation shall the raging flame sear;
our horrendous obligation to the insolent majority andras subspecies
now vanished for all infinity,
our bestowed creative intellect
and our invocation of entrepreneurship
can then reign with immortal impunity!

With the passage of celestial time,
earths' rule imposed will be divine,
the land and the seas shall rightfully metamorphose,
transforming back into their original deposed stock,
of course.

All the tarnishing poisons
from purgamen rudeness shall vaporize,
the wicked destitution all gone that the superlative despise.
The cluttered earth will become cleansed once more again,
the purloined space occupied by the rightful superlative then
the most abundant superior in nature shall once more propagate,
for the endowed supremacy in earth can no longer wait!

The love of all men shall be for their women,
and the adoration of both shall be for the children.
Their orientation shall be for strategic industrialization
and effective concluding organization,
repairing and replenishing the earth only shall be
the sole purpose for their propagation.

All of their motivations
toward progress in perfect harmony

with nature's timeless rhythm,
for the mutated gene for complacent waste
shall unto the furnace be given.
All of the land about will afford it's superlative best,
the mutated gene for inefficiency searing with all of the negative rest.
The newly freed space then organized into absolute efficiency,
all of the people dwelling in close apartment harmony
with both the land and one another,
everyone organized toward the progress and excellence of his brother.

Sickness and causeless pain shall then cease,
for the mutated gene engendering it will have found it's timeless peace.
Only the endowed wise will stand supreme,
for the mutated gene for fool and folly will be the subject of past dreams.
Heart wrenching heirloom illness and birth defects
will no longer have place among earths' new elect.
The mutated genes gone for a timeless infinity,
those once tearing mothers now dwell in the sweetest serenity.

When their wicked demigod shall be horribly crucified,
we will then know that the annointed time hath thus arrived.
Upon that mount our eternal instruction shall be given,
the positive motivations of those once reposed now living.

The glorious call for all to graciously arise
to follow the consecrated duty call by his brother's side.
All deteriorating complacency is to be despised.
No place for wasting talent or delaying time.

Then
during those most glorious of days,
the entire earth shall exist as an immaculate tropical garden.
The great plains of Alesia shall once again grow lush vegetation,

the mighty amber rivers of old shall now again flow;
the two main rivers, the *Fidi* and the *Ravdi*, that once flowed side by side,
each elbowing into a different direction at the same point,
forming an island called, *Sanctifacata Turbarum*, the hallowed place of gathering.

It will be here that the all powerful
Zorothausi
is predestined to lead those remaining,
eternally preserved by the encompassing crucible.

At the very point on that island all of the living will be judged
by the works of their hands and the visions of their minds.
The destructive negatives will then be weighed against the splendid positive.
Should the scale be found tipping against the positive,
then this individual will be deemed unfit for the kingdom Of God
and delivered headlong into the timeless purging furnace.

Following the astounding judgment,
where all dark secrets shall be brought into the light,
all the graves of earth shall then render themselves open,
the seas of earth shall offer up the remains contained therein,
no matter how small the fragments of dust,
the earth shall offer up the ash. . ..

From this matter will be thus garnished precious DNA
and other genetic material, presently known and unknown,
whereupon the dead shall be resurrected into their original superlative bodies.
At that very point of restoration,
all of their sins are instantly forgiven,
since they shall be restored into their original positive genetic superlative,
leaving the negative material inside the dust of the earth

to serve as nourishment for the new orchids
and luscious rose gardens of the succulent island menagerie.

All of the wicked vanquished
shall thus be rendered into nourishment
for the new tropical vegetation of earth,
and all of their ash scattered without,
from one farthermost corner into the other.

All tears shall thence be wiped,
all disease rendered into the dark passage of time.
The cruel twisted perplexities of mortal life then rendered simple,
engendering only pleasure and positive response.

" No more hunger,
no more pain,
no more useless labor,
no more vanishing gain,"
they all shall chant in perfectly synchronized unison!

At that divinely anointed time
those dreary forces of the sub-species numerical majority shall be
completely conquered.

All
of the nether mortals
and the vanara-men shall then
be reduced into rich plant nourishing ash,
since all of the negatives dramatically
outweigh the genetic positives.

This
colossal conflagration

shall come about immediately
following the crucifixion of their wicked demigod,
Magna Latro,
thenceforth *f*orever being consecrated
during the night of the great Walpurgis.

On
the glorious day of his capture,
a bleak veil covering the entire earth shall then be lifted.
His massive army of nine hundred thousand thousand
shall be captured and subdued
in a single outstanding move of superlative strategy,
further confirming the blessed identity of thy illustrious master,
Zorothausi!

From
the place of battle in greater Alesia,
he shall be dragged behind a line of seven sable war horses,
to the open plains of Megiddio
at the center of the earth.
High up
on mount *Theiko Vouno,*
on the massive granite *dome of eternal Knowledge,*
he shall be crucified,
with the entire world bearing witness.

The magnificent,
Zorothausi,
Great Lord Of The Conquering Superlative,
shall then turn toward the mighty east,
since this was the place of man-kind's origin,
offering a final extraordinary instruction unto all men.

As he speaks those cherished
words of instruction,
massive cerulean fire shall lash down from heaven,
alighting the crucified body of
Magna Latro,
the abomnible demigod of the nether mortals,
into an all consuming cyan flame.
The wrenching screams of his singeing torture
shall ring out to be heard by all the earth.

In this manner,
all will know that the Lord
of the immaculate endowed superlative hath surly returned!

With the permanent conquest of the nether-men forces,
all serenity and beauty shall be restored unto planet earth.
At the exact instance of the last remaining inferior body
being rendered into furnace flame,
the entire earth shall metamorphose into a superlative magnificence
more extravagant than the mortal mind can conceive
or the spoken words of mortal language can describe!

It is on this
precise moment that the great and wonderful
King of Kings,
Zorothrausi,
shall stand before all of superlative humanity restored,
congratulating them on their extraordinary efforts and success,
telling them all that surly man-kind
and all the earth has entered into a dawning celestial age
of supreme reasoning and enlightenment,
never before witnessed on the face of all the emerald earth
since the consecrated time of the original superlative.

To rule them temporarily
he placed his next in superlative command,
Mu
His reply unto them was that he must leave
to prepare a place for them even more magnificent than
the restored superlative earth,
since the earth was only the first half
of the prophesied restored Holy kingdom.

According to the most ancient of sagas,
he is predestined to return unto the original
Summus Nibiru,
to restore that outstanding supreme kingdom
back into the original superlative
that it was before the time of the great migration.

On that anointed day
he shall once more ascend to the summit of
Theiko Vouno,
raising both hands high in appeal unto
the reigning supreme Adonis of the skies,
Ahuramazda,
then he shall rise into the heavens,
vanishing from all sight a midst the low moving clouds above,
promising to return on an assigned anointed time.

THE DEVIL AND THE DARK TOWER

He was born
on the passing of the black sun,
the bane of daylight during the time of Capricorn.
The seat of his birth was behind the brilliance of Pergamon
scorned.

His wretched appearance
was of the gloomy subspecies-beast,
donned solely in putrid tatters torn;
he was raised in a shattered back alley possessing least
the ability to reason and pathetically shorn
of any creative deductive skills to extrapolate.. ..

Thus
he dwelt on the ragged streets among the cruelest beasts,
only motivated by forces of basic biology and
surrounding environment,
engaging in rancid purulent pursuits,
victimized by the most tarnishing debauchery...

Hence
he possessed no knowledge of distinction between
positive and negative,
but was only motivated toward debasing objectives,
since
such was the inception of his mutated directives.
With no deductive
check in place,
the need deduced by analytical logic,
the conclusion rendered thus bearing the surest way;

His life was only directed toward
domination by intimidation,
his motivation for ultimate power
among the lawless ward.

By the most putrid of tarnished craft
he ascended,
his throne among the streets dominating half
a dank dreadful kingdom
deeply desired by all of the vir-subspecies.

His enforced demand for fleshly favors
was soon to dominate,
the least tarnished religiously compelled
into his harlots' savor;
he cared not for those whom his desires could only motivate
into fumes of anger destined only to evaporate.

The deeply coveted sales routes
of the entrancing herbs and raptus pollen he was
destined to rule
by rude force of violence and
the dark power to intimidate.

In the freedom to torture
he assumed great enrapturing pleasure,
bearing the power through mere thought
of their dreadful
suffering should they fail to negotiate.

Consumed in arrogance,
fueled by an incessant insolence,
he soon roamed those luxuriant streets

bearing superlative opulence,
compelling the nether mortal masses
into systemic disharmony
with their genetic caste.

His blatant disregard
for sophistication and elegant social distinction,
born from unrestrained labor toward
an elaborately endowed conclusion.

Such disregard appearing,
served to court the nether mortal masses
by appealing into their covetous rearing
and base genetic direction.

Thus
their great discontentment was fueled
by his message' inception
and the dominating position that he held in
his throne among the putrid alleys of the tattered streets.
Had the position of logic
been in their extrapolate possession,
then they could have made the valid conclusion
to reject his dark rule
by power of deduction;

Hence
the exacting power of analytical deduction
would reveal his dark appeal to emotion
and all of their horrifying eminent destruction.
For the intellectual arts,
he held great disdain,
he cared not for artistic appreciation

nor those of whom develop the talent to obtain
the cherished creative skills.
His only motivations being those of the most basic biology
and those environmental extremes,
and his complete indulgence of the seven scelus courting calamity.
From the very onset
his negative rule is destined to conclude
with the ultimate negative
being the complete and conclusive destruction
of those among whom he was given rule.

But
they were compelled outside of their ability to contest,
since it was all programmed into their
constitution,
thus
a future consuming world conflagration is
inevitable,
bearing the absolute intention of halting
and reversing the total
putrefaction of all emerald earth.

Behold!
The varna-men and the nether-mortals
shall hail him as the
Great Giver Of Gifts,
Magna Latro!

He shall seduce millions by appealing
to their propagandized sense
of needing reparation from the hands
of the Superlative Grand.

"Was it not they,"
he shall say in his compelling sway,
"who held us in perpetual bondage,
forcing us into their service
day after loathing day,
only to purloin our precious heritage,
our endowed right to both prosperity
and play?

Are they all not
indebted to us for our lost time
in potential wealth,
for our abolished value potential in property
and health?
Did we not suffer dreadfully at their
hateful,
abusive hands,
as they struck us savagely to force us
to extract great wealth from their wretched lands?

Did they not abuse our sons
and daughters only to avenge our justified insolence
and insubordination?
And upon the very moment that they had won,
they only mercilessly forced us *all* to consume dung?
Is it now not *our* ranks who swell the more,
flourishing from on their brilliant abundance from
sea to glinting golden sea shore?

Behold
on this very day
let it be us to hold the sway!
Let us all arise and

then all wickedness shall melt away
before the astounded eyes
of all emerald earth!

Hence
I shall declare here unto the all of you,
that no power in all of earth or hell can halt our exalted advance!
So arise all ye reposing
beasts of emerald earth,
ascend by the thousand thousands into
thy brilliantly eminent berth!"

THE MOON

So
The time expended hath been thus;
we have labored dutifully
to entrust
thy blessed talent that hath been
dutifully invested in us.

Massive buildings we did
construct,
expansive boundaries we did
put up.
Soon
simple wards transformed into
parish pride,
then parish pride
transformed into provincial wonder,
then provincial wonder
transformed into instated glory,
instated glory
radiated forward into national
grandeur!

What were we then supposed
to do or think,
when the inferiors moved in
to tear down and sink?

I
eternally shutter when I speak these words,
for all who listen
have surly heard,

that goodness is like dew that glistens
in the new morning sun,
thus
the wicked love to christen
our heads with
a timeless presence just for fun!

Their decaying existence
hath infiltrated our gifted masses;
first
corrupting our lucid blood,
then our organizing entities,
infecting our enlightened academies once so divine,
finally our morals and then
our once illustrious minds.

Are we now doomed only to eternally fall
from thy divine grace?
Will the corroding wickedness ever be
forced into it's proper place?
What astounds the mind into disbelief,
is how quickly just a few can give into weakness,
and the destruction once in motion,
then knows no cease!

The longing taste,
once it has been sampled,
can then render itself insatiable,
even into the point of rendering
the strong body into rancid waste!

What saddens the watcher most,
is when the wise

among the wicked host,
refuse to acknowledge that which is to be despised!
Their only immediate reaction
being to boast
that the world still continues on
as time past has surmised.

Where then,
lies is the need for despair
and worry,
when time has thus no need to repair,
for the present only exists now
as it has in all time prior;
concerning the pain of initiating action,
why
there exists no need to hurry?

The tarnishing evil continues on,
thus
the individuals who seek corrective action
may never expect to succeed,
because
the few who have been entrusted with power
can never move when the majority
can mercilessly force our extraction,
forever damning the conclusive action
and the motivating will.

We loath the drudgery of our incessant servitude.
The villain always taking advantage of our inner motivation
toward perfectionist magnitude.
Our profit we are compelled by extortionist legality
to share,

by an alien reigning regime who only pretends
to care.

They play on the majority's inability
to adapt,
causing them to feel that we are held in dept
to them for their sustenance
and their purloined extravagant luxury.

They have been led that to be only payed
a basic wage,
that we have used them as pawns for our own gain,
playing them like fools held in a dark cage,
taking our sadistic pleasure from their wretched pain
into their extended austere decrepit age.

In all perfect truth
we were only engaged in our duty unto thy community
and thy nation,
. . ..forsooth!

Thy ruling elite is concealing their own crimes by vanity,
but ye are way to vain to comprehend
the vile insanity!
Of the plain facts ye blatantly refuse to view,
until the blood thirsty demon arrives at thy own house
to vilify you!

Until the base extortion equals seventy five percent,
and should ye, anon, cry aloud for mercy,
then deep into the laboring pen ye shall be sent!
Only again to toil without rest
in the name of nation state,

thy labor in quality held only unto the highest
standard rate among the best,
forced to submit unto their dark refusal to compensate.

Behold,
each and every time we held our heads high,
to walk in Lady Liberties' majestic illumination,
to rightfully bask in our earned wealth and status limelight,
the sin of covetousness consumed the nether mortals,
and our own traitorous elite became our most destructive blight.

During the days of our own time
we prospered unrestrained and our glory in wealth reigned supreme,
but then fell under sway of conquering empire,
our glitter only temporarily lost it's gleam.

Soon within the structure of their legal regulation
we were destined to rise again,
but their covetousness swelled
and their extortion grew when
they observed us consumed in our elegant assail.

With the passage of time
the repressive empire died,
and again we had risen to elegant divine,
only to be diminished by barbarians,
leaving us to only wonder as to why.

Soon our once lavish kingdom
was to rise again,
to conquer the world in the name of freedom,
allowing us to glitter once more,
like spectacularly delightful sin!

Then the covetousness of the sub-mortals
consumed all of the rule of law when
the new land to the West began.

The search for gold left the conquerors fuming,
but the wealth of the earth in entrancing herb
sparkled the eyes of our superlative human.
Thus by his own enterprise
he was to stun the astonished,
yes
among all that only spoke the telling word!

Into
the far east he was to ride,
searching only bearing true compassion in his heart
for the amendment of his compeer nether mortal,
to abide with the rule of the superlative law,
apart from the general goodness in his soul that thrives
within the genes of the positive superlative charge.

With the diligent search came the discovery of
those lost souls in such serious need,
that nourishment from their ranks
had evaporated without recovery,
hence
even their own flesh became game
and that of their own seed.

Thus
came the massive salvation effort,
their gracious congregations flowed
into their transporting container to afford
generous passage and decent abode.

According to their most ancient myths
those supreme gods from the heavens would return to save them,
transporting them into a congenial eternal bliss.
Through those superlative efforts
the answers to those heavenly requests manifested
from prayer time's distant mist.
By transport via heavenly vessels
they rode into their fabled paradise
with overwhelming zest!

Behold
in their new Elysium,
just as foretold in their fables of old,
all that was required of them was their labor
and of all the rest their cares could withhold.

Here
there was no more need to fear the bleak extremes,
or to anticipate the grip of starvation's hold,
or to flee the pursuit of some starving villains compelling supreme.
Their days and nights were planned ahead,
they were only born,
labored and fed,
continuing day into following day
until the hand of time found them dead;
then they were all given their respectful burial
in a most accommodating way .

As the joy
of the laboring nether mortals
consumed all time and productive space,
the

dawning wealth of the superlative swelled
until a precious glowing extravagance was the case.

The untalented
inferiors surrounding them in their unbridled covetousness grew,
appealing unto their elitist masters above them,
who only envisioned the abandonment of all liberty
that the land ever knew.

Soon came the call for battle
from the unjust as their jealousy grew,
the legions of the venara-men were to viciously lash out,
the sadistic rule of the many above the superlative few.

Though they battled brave,
consumed with an astonishing valor
and imagination that flowed in an outstanding wave,
still they wilted before the ceaseless billow,
but of the lucid blood and the precious vision
they did save.

Far away
near our most ancient of homelands,
the will and elaborate lifestyle of the superlative knew
the lavish taste and the spice of liberation
that raw imagination and talent blended can stew!

But
at the same time
those untalented disenchanted did whine
and the welling fury of covetousness rose too,
until their inferior majorities rushed out destroy
the only chance at liberty that they ever knew.

Today
the great tide against us continues,
just now what are the brilliant and talented to do,
only sit around and pine for times long lost,
wasting our precious lives with the jester being blue?
Or just pine away our time with the unproductive naught,
'cause the traitors will simply extort away our justified reward,
since the highly skilled and artistic are fraught
only with the superlative few?

SAGA OF THE RISING SUN: THE DELIVERING MESSIAH OF THE DIVINE MAGNIFICENT

According to the most ancient of sagas from the Volsungs,
and some suggested from the Mahabharata,
times in the most ancient past of man were simple and life proceeded thus:

In the beginning was the almighty
Ahuramazda,
who was here overseeing the massive chaos of the earth
during it's formative time.

Only the word was spoken
and the earth beneath the all encompassing sea began to rumble
and shake into a horrendous thunder.

The land mass then fragmented due to the colossal violence
and rose to the top of the seas,
forming dry land on eastern side
and then allowing the seas to flood the western side of the earth.
It was there on the eastern side,
that all of life began.

Life flourished here in an eternal complacency
with programmed success as it's ultimate destiny.
Then the forces of the superior positive decided
to place man into this glorified Elysium garden
of spiritual martyrs in the incessant celestial battle
between the superlative positive and negative.

The place they chose to allow man to initiate
was on the massive peninsula,
Solvognen.

This area was chosen as a result of in-depth scientific analysis
by the original superlative,
who originated from the planet,
Summis Nibiru.

According to their own legend,
they had fled their own planet due to over population
and excessive resource exploitation,
choosing earth because of it's astounding similarity
to their own home planet.

The great peninsula,
Solvognen,
was determined following in-depth analysis,
that both the land and the future colony
would benefit from having a band of islands scattered around it,
yet still within the general proximity.

As a result,
a massive asteroid was deflected
and caused to smash into the peninsula,
which forced it to break up
into a number of large fragments along the edges.

Three thousand years later,
when the earth had completely healed,
the colony was then effectively established.

At first the colony struggled for a while,
but then through inventiveness and outstanding industriousness,
the colony built itself up and began to prosper beyond imagination.

During those days of extreme prosperity,
the colonist constructed those most magnificent ruins
that are still found beneath the waves of the deepest seas and on land,
that astound the most knowledgeable of men,
even to this very day.

It is also known that these adventurous individuals
traveled around the entire globe
and established other colonies that flourished into unimaginable heights.
So all appeared to be extremely well in the beginning.
Some even going as far away as South America,
into Manta, for instance.
It is for that reason that the natives there unto this very day,
bear far more the appearance of the original superlative
than those from any other region within that distant realm.

Soon following the time of extraordinary rise into prosperity,
came the dreaded curse from the divisive lord of the negative superlative,
who became extremely envious of the success born by the positive
creation;

So in the beginning,
small family pockets of the positive superlative
begin to suffer as a result.
With the passage of time,
sufferings began to mount,
as was to be expected during the course of these situations;
and the people cried without end unto the almighty,

Ahuramazda,
for divine deliverance.

During the time of the exalted *Ennead Annual Tempus Immortales* celebration,
given on the vast plain of Alesia in *Sarmatia,*
at the time of the spring equinox for the twelve days of spiritual transcendence,
a rumbling voice on the midnight wind announced
the coming of their anointed divine deliverer unto the magnanimous masses of mortal earth
who gathered there for the immaculate spectacular celebration of flame and insensibility.

According to the voice of distant rolling thunder,
the divine deliverer was destined to be born at midnight,
during a strange but brilliant storm of fire and ice.

A phosphorus
rain of illuminating gold would fall following the glittering storm,
that would bear a singeing sting unto the exposed flesh of mortal men.
This rain would force his burro born parents to seek shelter in a cave
near the wilderness trail to the plain of Alesia,
on their way to pay an owed share in tribute to the supreme god,
Ahuramazda,
for his nine years of blessings
and abundance enjoyed by the people of earth.

The inside dimensions of the cave would be
twenty seven *sacred mina* (54 feet) by twenty seven.
Inside the cave on the eastern wall,
would be a cleft one *divine metra* (a cloth yard) by one *metra* in length,
and another by depth.
Above this natural cleft would be a fissure,

exposing the cleft to the air surrounding the hill containing the cave.
Within this fissure immediately above the cleft,
would be a smaller natural cleft
approximately one *glorious mina* (two feet) by another,
and another deep.
The inside of this prophesied cave would be where the divine couple
and their servant would seek shelter from the singeing rain.

Into the three by three cleft the divine couple
would place nine rounds of scrounged oaken driftwood,
alighting a comforting flame that eventually had to be fed again,
forcing the couple to exit the cave for more warmth producing driftwood.
The couple would remain inside the cave for ten full days
and nights,
with the sacred child being born on the eve of the fourth day.

Early that morning
the exalted father would exit the cave for more wood,
leaving the mother to sleep in sacred rest.
The servant was prophesied to place the anointed child into the cleft
immediately above the fire hearth.

Upon the exalted father's return,
great alarm would arouse concerning the sight of the child
comfortably asleep within the glowing stone above the hearth.
When he and the servant rushed forward to their astonishment,
a divine firmament of solid ice had formed to neutralize the heat of the flame
into the same surrounding temperature as that of the babe's flesh,
providing a very comforting rest.
This event would constitute the next sign of anointed divinity.

On the eve of the seventh day,
a coven of twelve lions would enter into the cave,
which they had been using as a den for the past seven years,
and instead of attacking,
they would bear gifts, including flesh:

Tyros or flesh of the bull,
Katsieka or flesh of the goat,
as well as *Pagoni* or flesh of the peacock and medicinal herbs,
laying them all simultaneously at the feet of the exalted family.

To further confirm the divinity of the babe;
one lioness would lovingly walk forward,
placing her own cub into the cleft where the babe lay,
which would sleep soundly as the babe himself.
This event would mark the final divine salutation,
heralding his future immaculate anointment as the delivering messiah.

As the child grew,
he by tack of demonstration,
would assume leadership of the anointed P*ainpestimo*,
or University of the S*ummum Intelligible.*
The wisdom of his escalier lectures was destined
to astound all of the most gifted wise men and scientists of his day,
causing them to anoint him as leader of the university entity by age twelve.

During this same period of time
he would lead the *league of the immortal twelve*
into realm of the *Koloss*, kingdom of the raging giants,
to defeat them in an outstanding show of strategy
and enrich the university of his employment with the plunder taken.

On the first day of his twenty seventh year,
he is predestined to call the genetic superlative
into heroic organized union,
for their rise into a supreme magnificence
that will endure
and prosper for thirty nine glorious years underneath his reign.
Thus he shall become the first woman born anointed divine king.

On the last day of his reign,
he and his entire kingdom shall journey
into the massive plain of Alesia,
in greater *Sarmatia*,
during the time of the spring equinox,
to pay homage unto the almighty god,
Ahuramazda,
where he shall announce that the moment has arrived
for his demonstration of supreme altruism
or *Theias Thysias*.

During this time he will choose the next reigning leader,
then request his own self sacrifice,
by first requiring that his sworn patron guards
throw him nude into a pool of freezing water,
whereupon being removed,
he will announce the final astounding proclamation to all men;
then he is destined to be cast into a pit of flowing lava,
where he will be absorbed into the realm of unseen mist.

In the distant celestial future,
when the specter of liberty,
intellectualism,
individualism and endowed artistic creativity,
as well as that of perfect reasoning and logic

shall vanish from the overwhelming majority of men,
who exist in a state of eroding genetic deterioration
into the intellectual and physical realm of the beasts,
he is predestined to return under
the same pretense as before in such conditions,
announcing his arrival for eternal salvation
of the very best among men.

The unseen spectrum of forces will place
the dividing crucible of technology
and fire upon all of mortal earth,
bearing the intention of separating the superior lucid minority
from the inferior mutated majority.

The majority will then cry unto their ruling authoritarian elites,
begging them for sustenance,
who will callously extort the sustaining funds
from the coffers of the endowed superlative.

After some time transpires,
the despairing superlative will cry unto the Almighty
for his delivering messiah to appear,
offering them his timeless relief.

During the time of the end,
he will raise the superlative forces
in their final show of outstanding supreme competence on mortal earth.

He will then move forward to annihilate the colossal,
numerically superior forces of
Magna Latro,
the dark demon possessed demigod of the nether-mortals,
crucifying him on the point of knowledge in the valley of Megiddo,

at the celestial center of the earth,
rising forth from that point to lead mortal earth
into a period of elegance and superlative intellectual,
creative genius un-imagined at any point in the entire history of mankind
or the immortal.

Hence forth,
for all transpiring eternity,
his name shall be known universally
as the great and mighty
Zorothrausi,

The Divine Deliverer,
son of the all powerful,
immaculate *Adonis,*
Ahuramazda!

THE JUDGMENT

And then,
that magnificent moment of endless waiting shall finally arrive!

Behold,
the sable thunder sun
shall transform into a now rising star
of dazzling fuchsia and luscious peach,
radiating across all of emerald earth with cozy embracing arms that
streak forth like jagged lightening bolts!

All of
superlative humanity shall stand before his enticing embrace,
savoring the seductive tranquility of his majestic radiation,
which not only soothes,
but heals all wounds and corrosive
manifestations,
knitting severed ligaments to bones,
broken bone back into solid,
and flesh back onto those now solid frames;

All of these marvelous blessings are freely granted,
while the inferior vanara-men and nether-mortals infecting our delightful earth
wreathe upon the dust of the ground,
screaming in dreadful pain at the singeing fury of the his incessant,
merciless anger.

Many thousand thousands shall lash out
into the void air surrounding them,
only cursing his holy name in vain,

being able to do nothing more for their own good
or toward the harm of superlative earth.

The earth shall then instantly open,
freely exposing all deteriorated remains,
from which the precious code of life shall be extracted
by the warmth of the enveloping suns rays;
and an advanced virtuous individual,
bearing a newly resurrected body,
shall arise forward into a radiating bedazzling perfection,
not witnessed since the days of the original ruling superlative.

At the same instant,
the depths of the seas shall deliver up it's remains,
all of the remains instantly restored into their original astonishing perfection.

Upon a distant throne of ice
illuminated by the rage of colossal enveloping flame,
is seated the immaculate form of the Almighty,
donned in the toga of flowing lustrous calcimine
and purpura,
bearing a sanctified laurel of prinus and holm.

In his right hand he bears
the anointed scales of celestial judgment,
in his left hand,
the sword of divine sacrifice
and punitive execution.

Forthright in extension from his person stands
the emaciated spectral figure,
Determinans,

in personification of the exalted superlative trinity,
being cherished sovereignty, immortal tenacity, and indomitable fortitude.

His complete anointed form
shall bear the supreme source
and superior example in personification,
endorsed in the spectrum of altruistic liberty
and superlative creative endeavor.

ANNONTIO!
That same astonishing spectrum has risen forward
to expunge repression
ever since those distant days of the original superlative,
forcing it's own separation from the repressive
negative surrounding;
then by force of shear audacity and persistence,
arises to initiate it's own illustriously designed realm that solidly
guarantees it's own right to superlative success won by
the fruits of it's own forthright initiative.

On the left hand side of the scales
bears the finite negative,
the right hand side of the scales
bears the infinite positive.

If the done deeds of hand and
creative intellect of mind
shall bear more of the positive on the celestial scale of life,
then that individual is free to savor the timeless blessing
in the dawning kingdom of the superlative infinity;
but
if those scales should tip into the left side,
then that individual shall be cast headlong

into the celestial purging flame,
serving faithfully to rid the superlative emerald earth
of his infecting consuming presence
for all time into infinity.

Behold
when the very last infected body shall be cast into the incessant flame,
the looming repressive veil upon mortal earth
shall then be lifted,
exposing an Elysium environment more fantastic
than even the most creative mortal intellect could
ever conceive of!

In the shimmering distance
of the vast Sarmatran plain shall illuminate the
astonishing sign of the superlative,
being the immaculate cross of Saint George
underneath the sickle moon reigning supreme to the lone tree of palm,
and the divine golden central ring of fire!

Before this beatifying sign,
all of resurrected superlative earth shall kneel
in complete consecrated homage to the Almighty,
for his generous endowment in restored superlative life,
swearing the sacred heart's pledge of enduring loyalty
unto that emaciated phantasm,
Determinans.

In the far distance
looms the sound of continuing rumbling thunder,
creating a massive swelling cloud of all encompassing dust;
the unified realm of emerald earth is soon consumed.

When the cloud shall lift,
all eyes shall behold a rejuvenated earth
and an exhilarated realm of true heaven,
a realm completely void of all negative,
within and without,
of both in flesh of body
and spirit form of misty soul.

In the midst of the raging rumble
shall battle the forces of the negative superlative,
wedded into the now deceased body of
Magna Latro,
causing his once dead corpse to spring forth
into what appears to be rejuvenated resurrected invigorated life.

Upon the very moment
that the cloud of dust recedes,
both he and his restored negative forces shall suffer
an all consuming defeat,
all then being bound and cast into the raging furnace
for time into exalted infinity!

No more will
superlative earth be forced to
submit unto the whims of the negative,
allowing them to reap the precious reward
while the righteous suffer the damning emanations!

No more
will superlative labor
be extorted for a loathing store,
only to be savored by insolent non-productive hoards,

who act out of some vain mythologized belief in
superlative indebtedness!

No more
will the superlative innocent
suffer due to the forced exposure of their youth
to the diseased squalor,
filth and tarnished blood of the nether-mortal inferior,
only to be despised by the remainder of emerald earth,
and even those of his own kindred!

The praying masses of superlative humanity
now gloriously arise,
facing the marvelous flaming cross of Saint George
and the illuminating center ring of fire,
with the astounding image of the thunder sun radiating
from behind the looming cross standing so proudly on the shimmering
distance. . .,
and that most majestic throne of judgment over looking the vast
plain from the far right hand side. . . . .

Before that brilliant cross stands a vast multitude,
numbering more than the stars of heaven
and the sands of the seven seas.

With their
right hands they raise the once forbidden
Bellamy Salute,
bearing sacred homage for the cross standing brilliantly before them.
In rigid formation
they stand,
now placing their right hands
tightly by their side.

In complete unison
they do an about right face,
toward the majestic throne of supreme judgment,
speaking aloud in near musical rhythm. . .

"Hail to thy superlative greatness,"
they chant in perfect unison.
"We submit unto thy endowed majesty,
for it was thee who created all surrounding,
and thee who gave us marvelous life in accordance to thy
gracious altruistic intrinsic generosity!

We hereby
commend ourselves into thy divine omniscient command. . .,
Hail unto thee
and the infinite march of the Superlative Grand. . .!"

THE BLISSFUL WORLD AND THE FOOL

ANNONTIO!
All is well in *Mundus* today,
the Divine Magnificent is ruler supreme!
The universe complete is presently at our controlling sway
and intrepid command,
I scream!
Now we may direct our resources toward
vast exploration
of nether worlds and exotic people,
offering elements bearing intrinsic wealth in alluring alien land.

Let the immortal bells of freedom
ring!

I
boldly herald
those songs of new wisdom
and sing
of the dawning time when creativity
shall bear no more repressive limitations,
and things
that engender astonishing manifestations
born from inspiring words
that bring
weight and substance,
rather than only dream
of what reality can never fathom
nor manifest
from thy precious time dutifully invested.

What progressing technological manifestations

shall the outstanding earth soon behold?
What
treasures shorn from sublime worlds abroad
may be shown to astonish our kind,
with welling desire for their possession
when they are sold!

What
skills are we soon to learn,
since we now possess the wealth
and time to scheme and plot
how we are to come to term
with those distant sources
of sublime knowledge got
from more illustrious beings on some
celestial Terra firm?

With
genetic drag from the nether-men now
permanently expunged,
we can serve to vastly improve our blood stock to endow
our vast future technological lunge!

From the scourge of inferior squalor
the natural earth is now eternally free
to grow and thrive abundantly from forest,
plain to hollow,
surging sea to golden sanded sea.

Now
ye granted relaxation amid thy surface dawning exposure,
thy fruits and vegetables divine may spread and be
delightful in thy composure!

No more chocking dust,
no more blinding smog,
no more waste of thy adored bounty entrusted
to the inferior squandering heaps
and their impenetrable fog.

Down with their
infected ruination,
those miserable lives
lived bearing no futuristic thoughts
nor positive convictions.
So now
lets indefinitely expose
the gracious yearning earth beneath
to the immaculate Adonis' radiant convection!

What new life forms wilt
thou then conceive,
what distant astonished minds will
beseech thee to believe?

What dawning
land forms will thy now retreating waters
then reveal,
when there exists no inferior presence
to make divine appeal
for thy majestic constructive efforts
to forebear?

ANNONTIO!
No
longer shall inferior beings belabor
thy divine creative efforts,

only to manifest thy
putrid desecration;
but
henceforth shall us superior labor
as thy supreme companion
to thy exalted exhilaration!

No longer
shall the incessant life forces of earth
forbear
their own exalted exhilaration,
only to accommodate inferior
substantiation!

Timeless
freedom and advancement shall henceforth
be our primary living rule!
Death
to both the oppressive extortionist tyrant
and the incompetent squandering fool!

Thy
luscious timeless wooded expanses shall
we anointed relish in our
rambling casual romp,
retaining our original composure of
blissful naive nymph in delightful tromp,
or cheerful passionate sprite in thy abruptly revealing enclosure.

Across
thy now resonate vine enshrouded
Bastille ruins,
our superlative roam in skillful illusions' way,

beholding those once gallant knights so bold,
instead of consternation's sway,
born from a repressive regimes' intimidating hold.

Our
timeless companions once again
shall be the cheerful cony,
the rail,
and the fawning hart,
for it was us among them where
we once dwelt right from the very start.

THE EXALTED CONCLUSION

Then,
so shall it all be.
The warm enveloping,
now purple,
thunder sun shall extend his rays
upon the face of all the earth.

And the future of the resurrected immortal
shall extend into all infinity,
with all singing praises
to the heavenly Adonis,
while consumed within the congregation
of the dawning translucent blood
of the most divine.

For all of blessed infinity
their songs of majesty
and praise shall ring forth throughout
the entire universe,
singing,
"praise be to the glory of Almighty God
and his anointed son,
blessed be the sound of their names
and the absolute perfection
in the resurrected redemption of earth."

Their pleasure shall know no limitations,
either in the physical world,
nor in that of the celestial intellectual realm.

Then all of the entire heavenly universe
shall sing and shout;

"Glory to them on high,
let eternal peace
and abundance be the rule that abides
Hosanna unto all that thrives,
Amen and Amen!"